Every Body Remembers

Do "The Work" and Get Past Your Past

Uncover and Restructure Negative Thinking Beliefs and Anxious Memories

Kimberly Davidson

Contents

Every Body Remembers   5

Part One: The Work-Up

1.   Your Journey of Hope, Help and Healing   13

2.   Childhood Disrupted   22

3.   Understand the Mind—Body Connection   36

4.   The Memory Zone   48

5.   Think Straight   59

Part Two: The Work-Out

6.   Techniques to Help You Through *The Work*   70

7.   Identify an Early Origin Memory in 6-Steps *(Session 1)*   81

8.   Detect Your Greatest Negative Thoughts and Beliefs in 3-Steps *(Session 2)*   91

9.   Change a Negative Thought and Belief in 6-Steps *(Session 3)*   99

10.   Update and Renew an Early Origin Memory in 6-Steps *(Session 4)*   115

11.   Befriend and Pamper God's Temple   139

Appendices

Appendix A: *Glossary of Terms*   153

Appendix B: *The Feeling Wheel*   154

Appendix C: *The Brain (Images)*   155

About the Author   157

References   167

Every Body Remembers

Might you be one of the walking wounded?

- Would you say your thoughts are ruling your life?
- Do your memories have control over you?
- Do you go to great lengths to attain affirmation you desperately crave?
- Growing up did people in your family say hurtful or insulting things?
- Ever feel like an important person despised and/or rejected you?
- Did you experience physical, sexual, or emotional abuse?

If you answered yes to any of these questions, this Work-book is for you. Most likely you've never made the connection between a *past adverse event* and a *present-day anxiety or fear.*

Ever notice you can get on a bike and automatically remember how to ride it, even if it's been years since you rode a bike? This is because *your mind remembers everything.* Sounds, smells, touches, tastes. A memory is not only locked somewhere in the recesses of your brain, it's also held in your body, all the way down at the cellular level.

(The way a mom treats her baby early in life literally affects which DNA gets transcribed, and therefore, the physiological path the baby's brain and body will take in life.[1])

Neuroscientists across America report that when an experience has deeply wounded us, the images associated with that experience, along with the emotions we felt at that time, *are forever attached together,* called a memory. These aversive memories can create unconscious deadly thinking and debilitating illnesses which takes over and structures our entire world. Stress early in life catches up with us when we're adults by altering our bodies, cells, even our DNA.

"Time conceals. Human beings convert adverse and traumatic emotional experiences in childhood into organic disease later in life," said Dr. Vincent J. Felitti, a pioneer in his field.[2] Yet, when people go to a therapist, they don't usually come in declaring, "I need help because my father didn't love me as a kid." They seek help because something they're feeling, thinking, or doing in the present is hurting themselves and their relationships. When people seek medical treatment, they don't proclaim, "My horrible past is wreaking havoc on my body today." They come in because their body is telling its story.

Past Memories are Very Much Alive

There's an old American Indian saying, "You can't out run what's inside you." The fact is: *Most of us are living a lie we were told about ourselves.* Behind every anxious and uncomfortable feeling, there's a thought that isn't true for us, and there's a memory that needs to be exposed and treated.

Even though something happened long ago, we usually don't recognize how much a stored memory still affects us today—mentally, physically, spiritually, and relationally. *The past stays present.* By choosing to look back, I unlocked several memories of relocating to a foreign country, and then to several new schools, as well as a number of parental pressures put on me. I recognized my dominant feelings were fear, loss of control, insecurity, and helplessness, which I carried into adulthood.

I never connected my eating disorder in adulthood to the anguish I felt as a kid moving each time—the fear I had about myself being "different" or not being liked. Not receiving healthy attention from my parents, teachers, and peers made me believe I didn't belong anywhere. Hence low self-worth and a negligent self-image emerged, leading into the world of negative thoughts and beliefs, and addiction. In counseling there's a saying that goes something like, "The gun was already loaded and cocked (referring to genetics); then one day a bad experience squeezes the trigger—then all hell breaks loose." Nature meets nurture.

My stored memories of rejection set me up for failure in my jobs. For the majority of my career I worked as a marketing representative. I got hired because of my ability to connect with people. Yet, every time I had to make a presentation or a sale, I'd get anxious and retreat to food or cigarettes to calm myself down. Why the anxiety? Fear of being rejected. Where did that fear come from? My childhood. I carried around numerous *untreated wounds in the form of "stuck" memories.*

Consequently, I've been diagnosed with several autoimmune disorders: lupus, prediabetes, adrenal fatigue, granuloma annulare (a skin condition that consists of raised, reddish lesions that forms ring patterns usually on the hands and feet), as well as shingles and gastritis.

Our takeaway: The brain is an incredible processing machine that digests and organizes everything we experience. But an adverse event, or any trauma, can overwhelm the brain's natural ability to process it, leaving behind pieces of the trauma, frozen in an unprocessed state. In addition, the immune system (the body's master operating control center) becomes oversensitive to threat, so it is prone to mount a defense, even when it means attacking the body's own cells. I find it ironic that, say, some person traumatizes us, then our own body reacts by assaulting itself.

What happens in childhood sets up the lifelong programming for governing the body, brain, and mind—the soul.[3] There are mental files of beliefs and memories governing your life today. Healing will be more difficult if you do not recognize that your past plays a strong hand in any physical and mental health problems you may have today.

The Work: Logos-Therapy

The beginning is never the beginning. In order to move forward, there must first be an ending. Otherwise we merely accumulate emotional baggage and carry our burdens from one situation to another. Perhaps a lot of our struggle to get past what we'll never get over is that we try to get a fresh start before we put an end to the past. … Perhaps our attempts to change have been frustrating or ineffective simply because we skip the step of avoiding the uncomfortable time of transition and turbulence associated with change, and jump right over to "new beginnings." … Endings are fearful. I am not at all comfortable with the frightening "in-between" stage where healthy change occurs. I like the idea of change; it is the changing I struggle with.

–Pastor John Westfall, *Getting Past What You'll Never Get Over*

We will never be free in any area of life that we're not willing to confront. Self-examination is an important part of living as an authentic Christian. Through The Work you will be guided to uncritically observe what you are experiencing: thoughts, emotions, memories, and body sensations—all with the goal of turning down the stress response, and reducing the intensity of toxic thoughts, beliefs, and memories. You will be equipped with some powerful Bible verses and time-tested counseling tools to help you get unstuck from the past so you can move forward towards the glorious plan God has for your life.

I call this work *Logos-therapy* (my own term; not to be confused with "Logotherapy" which focuses on the meaning of human existence). The gospel of John defines Jesus as *the Logos*—the very agent God used to create all things (John 1:1-2). *Logos* is translated "the word of God." *Logos-therapy* is an integration of Scripture, psychology, and education. Logos-therapy helps people not only identify their issues, but develop a new way to process daily problems and live as Christ designed.

I believe 2 Timothy 3:16-17 which states, *"All of Scripture is God-breathed."* While some parts of the Bible address cultural norms that don't apply to today, Scripture, or "God's Word," is the authority for my life and the foundation of Logos-therapy. Time and time again God uses His Word to breathe encouragement and hope into His children's lives. It's where God meets us. *"For everything that was written in the past was written to teach us, so that through the endurance taught in the Scriptures and the encouragement they provide we might have hope"* (Romans 15:4).

Turning to the Bible in a time of crisis or pressure may feel like an unnatural response—but it is the path that makes most sense since God created every one of us and knows us inside out. Or, perhaps you may feel resistant because Scripture has been used against you in the past, made you feel judged or guilty. That wasn't God. It was the enemy.

When we go "by the Book" we will find wisdom, healing, peace, even joy, a supernatural power. The words in the Bible have way more authority than what I say or write. Give the "Good Book"—God—the benefit of the doubt.

The advantage of exposing ourselves to Scripture is we can declare truth over our difficult situations. For example, *"The LORD nurses them when they are sick and restores them to health"* (Psalm 41:3); *"I [God] will give you back your health and heal your wounds"* (Jeremiah 30:17). It also helps us identify problematic thoughts and beliefs, like putting on corrective lenses. We see more clearly and from God's perfect perspective.

Martin Luther said, "The soul can do without everything except the word of God. We must allow the Word of God to confront us, to disturb our security, to undermine our complacency and to overthrow our patterns of thought and behavior."

God promises, *"You will know the truth, and the truth will set you free"* *(John 8:32)*. The Bible proclaims, *"Christ has truly set us free. Now make sure that you stay free, and don't get tied up again in slavery …"* *(Galatians 5:1)*.

If we desire true freedom, we need to stay close to God and follow His instructions, lest we get tied up in slavery again. And we can always pray what St. Augustine prayed, "Lord, give me what you are requiring of me."

The Perfect Counselor

"Jesus stopped and called, "What do you want me to do for you?" *(Matthew 20:32)* He's asking you the same thing. What is your response?

We talk to ourselves and each other about our problems when we should be talking to Jesus about our problems. He is *the one* who does the real work in us; He's the force for transformation; He's the Perfect Counselor—God who became flesh (John 1:1-3;14). As a man, He agonized, wept, and knew temptation, betrayal, and loneliness. He needed the power of God's love—just as we do. He is one of us! He gets us. His association with frail humans allowed Him to understand their pain, empathize with their weaknesses and enter into their suffering.

Jesus displayed extraordinary perception and sensitivity to read a person's heart, *"For he knew what was in a man"* *(John 2:25);* *"he too shared in their humanity"* *(Hebrews 2:1)*. Today, He is in tune to *your* feelings; to *your* disappointments, brokenness, fears, and sorrows. Our heart's cry needs to be, "Lord, help me and change me."

Jesus said, *"Here on earth you will have many trials and sorrows. But take heart, because I have overcome the world* *(John 16:3)*. There is no perfect road map for the journey through pain and loss. Yet, there is always *hope.* Matthew 14:36 tells us, *"They begged him* [Jesus] *to let the sick touch at least the fringe of his robe, and all who touched him were healed."*

Jesus Christ is God which means His spirit is everywhere and living in every Christian. He doesn't call us to a task without equipping us for it. After all, have you read in the Bible something like, "and then God failed them"? No. God is in charge, and there is nothing more exciting than stepping out in faith to watch the Healer and Counselor work in our minds and hearts. He is our greatest ally, the most powerful resource for recovery, and totally on our side in our struggles.

(If you are confused between who God is and who Jesus is, and how they can both be God, see this note.[4])

✝ ✝ ✝

This Work-book is not intended to take the place of medical or psychological care. For some of you, this will be all you need. Many women after taking this class and learning to open up, breathe a sigh of relief. They understand the reason for their pain and realize they are not "crazy." For others this may be one part of your overall healing plan.

Healing timelines and responses vary from person to person.

The Work does not come with a 100% healing guarantee. Complex medical issues and trauma require more than the tools we explore in this book. Licensed clinical counselors are trained to treat the difficulties associated with emotional pain. *It's okay to not feel okay; there's no shame in seeking help.*

If you're feeling depressed or extreme distress and/or are in therapy for a complex traumatic problem, or feel you might have one, such as PTSD or an anxiety disorder, please don't do the suggested exercises in Part Two unless a therapist clears you to do so. Certainly, use the material in Part One to understand yourself better.

If you are in a group, some women who have a history of trauma can take on the emotions of the group and feel re-traumatized. Again, pray and decide what is the best course of action for you.

If you feel suicidal, seek help immediately. Call 1-800-273-8255 or 911

Part One: The Work-Up
Know Thyself

My dear daughter-in-law knew I was struggling and suggested I see a counselor that she and her mom had been seeing. It's a bit unsettling when your daughter-in-law suggests you see a counselor, but I was feeling desperate so I agreed. What else did I have to do with $70 an hour?

I dressed up for my first appointment. (I didn't want to look like I needed counseling). I was a little nervous when I arrived but was met by a very nice young man who quickly put me at ease.

At the end of the third session he said he didn't think I needed to come back again. This surprised me as I thought it was just getting good. Really? That's it? (I think I might have rolled my eyes.) I was totally unprepared for what he told me.

"Annie, I see a nicely dressed woman who seems to be handling life fairly well. For the last three weeks you have come in wearing well-fitting masks. However, there are a few cracks in those masks and I see light behind them—light you are not letting out. From what you've told me about growing up with alcoholic parents, I understand the reasons for the masks. But your parents quit drinking long ago and those reasons don't exist anymore. I want you to start removing the masks and begin to let the light out. It's time."

For once I didn't know what to say. I just sat there wide-eyed.

He went on, "Let me tell you what I see behind the masks. (I really didn't want him to tell me.) I see a little girl slouching with her shoulders hunched, protecting her heart. To open her heart meant she would need to really care about others. To step outside herself and be open and vulnerable. She could be hurt or frightened or confused or embarrassed. *Too risky*. So, she's been guarding her heart all these years. I see a little girl with her head down, afraid to make eye contact. She's afraid to really connect with people. That would take her out of the safe world she has created. People might be too needy, they might ask too much of her, or they might reject her. *Too risky*. So, she's been keeping people at arms-length all these years. I see a little girl with clenched fists. (I looked down and mine were.) If she opens her hands she would have to reach out and touch others. She would have to feel the world around her. *Too risky*. So, she's kept her fist clenched all these years. I see a grown woman full of light with so much to offer. Annie, it's time to let your light out. The world needs what you have. Your masks aren't super-glued on but they won't fall away instantly either. Begin to connect—to yourself and others. Trust my advice."

By now, I was a mess. Trying hard not to cry. I could see the little girl, too. I managed to say "Thank you," and gave him his check for $70. I cried all the way home (not a safe thing to do).

God wanted me to shine my light, His Light, and I had been hiding it behind masks all these years. That was the best $210 I ever spent!

"And he [Jesus] said to her, "Daughter, your faith has made you well. Go in peace. Your suffering is over" (Mark 5:34).

–written by my good friend Annie Paden, author of *Fruit Flies*

✝ ✝ ✝

L. B. Cowan wrote in her devotional, *Streams in the Desert,*

You must be willing to take your ideas of what the journey will be and tear them into tiny pieces, for nothing on the itinerary will happen as you expect. Your Guide will not keep you to any beaten path. He will lead you through ways you would never have dreamed your eyes would see. He expects you to fear nothing while He is with you.

1

Your Journey of Hope, Help and Healing

Time heals all wounds is a lie.

Rose Kennedy agreed and wrote, "The wounds remain. In time, the mind, protecting its sanity, covers them with scar tissue, and the pain lessens. But it's never gone." The problem is we think we've moved on, but then something triggers that scar-tissued wound, and there it is again—right up front. One of the greatest American writers, F. Scott Fitzgerald felt the same way, "There are open wounds, shrunk sometimes to the size of a pin prick, but wounds still."

The past remains present is the truth. Things happen to all of us that we don't get over.

Clinicians have found that the primary cause of toxic thinking and out-of-control behavioral reactions is due to experiences that have been stored in the brain as unprocessed memories. Think of a memory as a box that contains every thought and belief associated with an event. Every thought you think is attached to a memory; every memory is attached to a present-moment feeling, which produces a reaction and behavior.

- *Event* → creates an *Image* in the Brain = *Memory*.
- Memory → creates *Thoughts and Beliefs*.
- Feelings, reactions and behaviors. →
- Run our lives—*emotionally, physically, spiritually, and relationally.*

It's like we've got these raw memories that are locked in a trunk that today reveal themselves as pervasive negative thoughts and feelings such as sadness, anger, fear, shame, anxiety, and resentment.

What I learned from psychiatrist Bruce Perry is that *we don't forget or get completely over adversity and trauma—but we can learn how to diminish its effects and carry it in a healthier way.* As broken, fallible humans living in a shattered world; we all have had significant injuries. There's always some sort of memory or flashback of the wound; some kind of sensitivity and trigger. But the power of that wound can lessen with time. Then we can learn how to use our experiences in a good and productive way.

Jon Kabat-Zinn wrote, "You can't stop the waves, but you can learn to surf." While we don't have the power to directly obliterate or magically change our thoughts, emotions, and memories, *we have the ability to change the image with which our emotions are associated.* How? By carefully choosing and adding new experiences that will create new neural structures and rewire old brain pathways effectively and safely, thereby creating renewed positive thoughts, beliefs, and memories. This is what The Work is all about. I should say, this is what God's Work is all about.

God promises to work our pain into a new exciting plan, *"See, I am doing a new thing!"* (Isaiah 43:19).

An Unexamined Life is Not Worth Living

Scars have the strange power to remind us that our past is real.

— Cormac McCarthy, All the Pretty Horses

As a new believer, I had been spiritually transformed, but emotionally and physically, I remained pretty much the same—stuck. I needed to get "unblocked" so the flow of the truth of God's Word and His Spirit could get into the crevices of my brain, mind, heart, and soul.

Many people believe "let sleeping dogs lie." In other words, leave things as they are—in the past. It's easy and comfortable. In his letter to the Philippians, the apostle Paul did say he is, *"Forgetting the past and looking forward to what lies ahead"* (3:13). The biblical word "forget" in this context doesn't mean "put out of one's mind." It means *letting go—not allowing the past experiences to dominate the future.*

Plato said an unexamined life is not worth living. What I can tell you from a counselor's perspective is that a buried past can not only be lethal to our overall health and our relationship with humans, but it can mar our relationship with God. *This is why it is critical to seek God's truth so a past stuck memory can be updated with accurate and truthful information.* By understanding how our past experiences lay the groundwork for our emotional and physical reactions today, we can find our "stuck" points and do something productive about them.

We get a picture of an unprocessed past from the psalmist in Psalm 43, *"Why am I discouraged? Why is my heart so sad?* This man is completely disheartened, which is what untreated memories can lead to.

Then he prays to God, *"Send out your light and your truth; let them guide me. Let them lead me to your holy mountain, to the place where you live."* Notice what he asks for: light and truth.

Jesus declared, *"I am the light of the world. ... I am the way, the truth"* (John 8:12; 14:6). The psalmist wraps up his prayer by declaring, ***"I will put my hope in God!*** *I will praise him again—my Savior and my God!"*

The thing about hope is it's tied to the act of surrendering to God. Surrender means transferring our need for power, control, and authority over to God, and resting in His perfect power, control, and authority. Don't run away; trust Him. He created us with the ability to bring ourselves back from the edge of chaos. God is closer to your soul than you are. Trust His examination and healing process.

God promises, *"I have said what I would do, and I will do it"* (Isaiah 46:11). You can put your hope in your Creator.

A Journey to the Center of Your Soul

One of Dorothy's classic lines in the *Wizard of Oz* is, "Toto, we're not in Kansas anymore." It will feel like you've left Kansas; left home. You are going on a journey with God! The crux of our healing journey requires challenging long-held thoughts and beliefs by choosing to root them out of our unconscious.

Catherine Booth, founder of The Salvation Army, once said, "If we are to better the future, we must disturb the present." You could say we're choosing to be 'short-term distressed' so we can be 'long-term healthy.'

Of equal importance—listen to your body and note any physical reactions and/or sensations. *The body speaks the mind.* When we experience any stressful bodily sensation—*there is a specific thought and memory causing our reaction, whether we're conscious of it or not.* The mind is connected intricately to the body. Our body becomes the entity that shows us through illness and disorders, what we are unconsciously ignoring, denying, dissociating, or repressing. It can give us valuable information to help identify what's running our world.

With God's guidance and by implementing proven techniques, we will be treating our mind and body by examining and processing our primary *negative thoughts and beliefs*, which I refer to as *NTBs*, and their associated locked up memories.

It's like an iceberg. The view from the surface of the water represents what we are consciously aware of—just the tip. The largest part of the iceberg is under the surface which represents thoughts, beliefs, and memories we are unconsciously unaware of.

The Work begins at the tip of the iceberg. As you move through the exercises you will be coached to go under the surface to access hidden parts of the iceberg. You will not be instructed to go back and relive your past; only asked to remember certain events so that particularly pervasive thoughts can be changed in a positive direction.

You can decide what sorts of modifications you want to make to increase your comfort level. In chapter 11, *Befriend and Pamper God's Temple,* we look at certain lifestyle changes to enhance and maintain total body restoration. If you have extra time, I encourage you to start reading this chapter and begin implementing the wellness tips.

Schedule a Work Appointment with Jesus

In order to avoid getting flooded by your emotions, I suggest "scheduling" reading time and processing your emotions. Create a specific time to meet with the Perfect Counselor Jesus. Make it *a prayerful appointment*. Then when you're done for the day, go back to what's going on in the present world.

Philippians 4:6 says to *"pray about everything."* In other words, "talk to Jesus about everything." Speak to Him as if He were physically present. His Spirit is close and leading you through the process. Don't be afraid to express *anything* on your mind. Remember, He already knows you inside out. Nothing is too trivial for Him to listen to.

If you feel too overwhelmed to pray, Romans 8:26 guarantees,

The moment we get tired in the waiting, God's Spirit is right alongside helping us along. If we don't know how or what to pray, it doesn't matter. He does our praying in and for us, making prayer out of our wordless sighs, our aching groans" (TM).

Pray for clarity and wisdom, and the removal of all distractions, before you start. Each day, or every other day, set your timer for anywhere between 30 to 60 minutes. If you are part of a healing group, consider group time your appointment for the day. Eliminate as many distractions as possible. (Turn off your phone!)

This is consent to feel fully the contents of your own heart without censorship or guilt or alteration. If you are hurting, then hurt. May you feel permission to cry, to grieve, to be not alright. May you relieve yourself of the burden of pretending everything is fine or faking stability or concealing the damage. May you feel not a trace of guilt for any twinge of pain or anger that seizes you today. Above all, may you find encouragement even in your profound anguish. May you find in your very sadness, the proof that your heart though badly broken, still works. *–Unknown*

End your time by thinking on a pleasant memory and thanking Jesus for something. The next day dive back in to continue The Work process. If unwanted thoughts come outside the scheduled time, tell yourself, "I have other things to do now. I will think about this during my next scheduled time." (Yes, this can be a challenge.) There are no right ways or rules.

Write to Heal

We can begin healing by opening our perspective and speaking truth through "Writing to Heal" exercises and journaling. Writing can be an emotional outlet, and form of prayer, that does something no other form of expression can do. Numerous sources report that 20-minute writing sessions about emotional topics, on consecutive days, reduced PTSD symptoms, depression, and anxiety after two weeks.[5] Writing has been clinically associated with improved health.[6] One counselor calls it *taking out our emotional trash*. You can use *The Feelings Wheel* in Appendix B to help you express yourself.

Many of us are concealing anger. Consider what Dr. James Dobson wrote, "The human mind cannot tolerate depression and grief indefinitely. The personality will act to protect itself in time, throwing off the despair and groping for stability. One method is by turning pain into anger."

Anger is a God-given emotion that helps preserve human life and relationships. Where it is not expressed, there exists a relationship that cannot manage normal stress. Anger, as intentioned by God, communicates feelings, perspective, beliefs, and desire. It protects, defends, and moves us to action. It also expresses jealousy. It is a *very normal* part of losing something that we love or need deeply. And feeling mad at God is normal too. *Why did God let this happen to me? How can He be a God of love if He lets people get away with such horrendous abuses? How come God does nothing about this situation?*

You are being given permission to express your anger. Typically, one of the primary emotions, like fear, loss, or sadness, can be found underneath anger. Shame, guilt or helplessness can also get buried under the anger, which is why we need to examine these emotions and thoughts so we can resolve these feelings and issues.

Psalm 62:8 says, *"Trust in him at all times. Pour out your heart to him, for God is our refuge."* I encourage you to write—pour out your heart—to God for at least 15 to 20-minutes a day, just like this psalmist, *"Have compassion on me, LORD, for I am weak. Heal me, LORD, for my bones are in agony"* (6:2).

Ask God your deeper questions and write down what you believe He is saying to you so you can remember His response. Many find they begin writing about things they hadn't consciously thought about for years, and come to see their situations differently through writing. You are recording your journey *"into a permanent record to be remembered forever"* (Exodus 17:14).

Akin to journaling would be painting, drawing, arts, or music. It's amazing how music has the power to make us smile, cry, go back to a pleasant time, or inspire us to dance!

Cultivate Self-Compassion and Grace

Have you noticed that we don't criticize or treat badly people we care for and love? Yet, that's often our mantra for ourselves. It's important to practice being an unconditionally kind, helpful, and encouraging friend to yourself. Just knowing you're doing the work and surviving the day shows immense courage and determination.

Start by giving yourself grace. For example, if you've sought comfort in food, alcohol, drugs or other addictive behaviors, remind yourself you were merely trying to escape negative feelings. The impulse made sense at the time, and it may have been the best mechanism that you had available at the time. Recognize if you struggle with anxiety that it is trying to keep you safe during a tumultuous time.

In other words, *accentuate the normality of your experience*. Don't forget multitudes of people in pain handle stress the same way. This is grace!

Let me also add that if you struggle with depression, you may believe the lie that your life has no purpose, which is simply not true. Try this: *Imagine you are a very compassionate, caring, and dedicated therapist.* You are walking "the wounded you" through a therapy session. Offer her compassionate and kind words, such as:

- I'm so sorry you had to go through that. That was horrible, yet you got through it. You're a survivor.
- I respect you for having the courage to ask for help.
- Everything you're thinking and feeling is completely normal. There's nothing wrong with you. You are an amazing woman!
- Jesus and I are here for you.
- *Add any caring statement in your own voice that feels authentic.*

The Work Roadmap

Our objective is to make sense of *a current experience*—a thought, a belief; perceptions and emotions—by delving into existing memory networks and then changing the trajectory. The Work will coach you through The Work-Up (Part One) and four sessions in The Work-Out (Part Two).

Part One: The Work-Up

This is your "classroom" time. Think of it this way: Before a doctor operates, he/she must have adequate schooling. Before we "operate on ourselves," we too must understand how God has created us.

There is truth to the old saying, "Knowledge is power." Even God says, *"My people are destroyed from lack of knowledge"* (Hosea 4:6). In Part One you will be getting to know how your entire body works—mind, brain, immune system, and more. Philosopher Baruch Spinoza once said, "If you want the present to be different from the past, study the past because to understand is to be free."

Part Two: The Work-Out

The Work-out is broken into four sessions. Each session includes a number of Work-steps:

> **Session 1:** Identify Early Origin Memories in 6-Steps
> **Session 2:** Detect Your Greatest Negative Thoughts and Beliefs in 3- Steps
> **Session 3:** Change a Negative Thought and Belief in 6-Steps
> **Session 4:** Update and Renew an Early Origin Memory in 6- Steps

Don't allow yourself to get overwhelmed. This journey is about new *habit-formation* and *transformation*, not information overload. The best definition I heard for transformation is "going back to God's original dream for us." What did God have in mind when He created you and me? What is His desire for us today?

We have an opportunity to take God's hand and experience the renewal and transformation of our minds, emotions, and wills through Jesus working in us. We're talking about creating new habits which will change our brains and lives profoundly, creating lasting recovery and emotional resilience.

This work is challenging but God will give you the ability to persevere. We are promised in 2 Peter 1:3, *"By his divine power, God has given us **everything we need** for living a godly life."* The words "has given" means it's already been done; past tense. This means we can live out Philippians 4:13, *"For I can do everything through Christ, who gives me strength."* Christ is sufficient enough for us.

Optional Prayer (Personalize as you feel lead)
Father, do you want me to proceed? Right now, I am feeling (*tell Him how you are feeling*). What do You want to do with my thoughts and feelings and memories? I receive your will. Thank You for being my Father and Perfect Counselor, and guiding me towards Your perfect plan. In Jesus's name I pray this.

> (*Listen. What good news is coming to your mind?*)
> *Respond:* I receive that Lord. In Jesus's name.

2

Childhood Disrupted

"I do not understand what I do. For what I want to do I do not do, but what I hate I do." Can you believe this is the super-apostle Paul speaking (Romans 7:15)?

How often have you wondered why you do the things you do? For instance, dating a person who treats you badly; getting angry at insignificant things. Or, do you do everything you can so people will like you and want to hang around with you?

Professionals state that those earliest and most disturbing memories are the key to our behaviors and many of our problems today. *Our brains don't forget.* Your memory bank is the cloud storage for your life's data. Like a super-computer, your brain receives and retains data from the outside world, compiling and maintaining a record of *every* event. Your complete story is in there; a world that no one else can see, touch or hear.

The Past Isn't the Past If It's Still Infecting the Present

What we know now is early adversities change the architecture of a child's brain. This, in turn, triggers an overactive inflammatory response for life, predisposing the child to mental health issues and adult disease. When a child is exposed to continual adversity and trauma, its effects can carry over into adulthood because their body is in a constant state of high alert.

Short-term, the stress response system serves a useful purpose. Short bursts are designed to save our lives. However, long-term, the adverse effects are harmful. God designed our stress response system to handle a very different set of stressors than the ones we face today.

The *Adverse Childhood Experiences Study*, referred to as ACE, is a study conducted by the Centers for Disease Control and Prevention and the U.S. Health Maintenance Organization Kaiser Permanente. (I will be using the acronym ACE which stands for *Adverse Childhood Experiences*.) ACE research discovered that 64% of adults have faced at least one harmful or traumatic event, and 40% faced two or more in their childhood. This means there's a lot of people struggling with psycho, social, and biological issues with "tuned-up" stress systems—people who most likely don't recognize their symptoms are rooted in damaging childhood experiences.

Research reveals that girls experience more adversity in childhood than boys; 50% of women are likely to develop anxiety and depressive disorders, and autoimmune diseases, in greater numbers than men.[7] Also, childhood trauma is an overlooked factor in the obesity epidemic. About 50% of obese patients report being sexually assaulted as children.[8]

Dr. DeLisa Fairweather, associate professor at John Hopkins School of Public Health and Mayo clinic stated,

> The link between being female, facing adversity in childhood, and later developing an immune disease is so consequential that it resembles the link between smoking and lung cancer, drunk driving and car accidents, and unprotected sex and pregnancy. … It takes time for inflammation and autoantibodies to cause damage to organs after a stressful event. A child can undergo chronic stress at 12-years-old, and it can take 30 years for the immune damage to progress to a clinically recognizable disease.[9]

Someone said, "You can try to run from your own wounds, but you'll leave a trail of blood behind." Consider the following questions:

- What was it like growing up in your family? *Dad drink? Mom cried? Grandpa died? Brother hit you?*
- What fears and shame-based feelings that you carry today do you believe came out of your family?
- How is your health?
- Have any health issues interfered with your life?

Take the ACE Survey

The ACE survey only identifies the "tip of the iceberg." Other types of toxic stress over months or years likely increase the risk of psycho, social, and biological issues. It doesn't consider adverse experiences outside of the family such as peer bullying, relocating, social media and sports pressures, or being rejected by other people. Let me add: Not all ACEs are about poor parenting. This ACE survey is merely a starting point.

Prior to your 18th birthday:

1. Did a parent or other adult in the household often or very often swear at you, insult you, put you down, or humiliate you? or Act in a way that made you afraid that you might be physically hurt?
No___If Yes, enter 1 __

2. Did a parent or other adult in the household often or very often push, grab, slap, or throw something at you, or ever hit you so hard that you had marks or were injured? No___If Yes, enter 1 __

3. Did an adult or person at least 5 years older than you ever touch or fondle you or have you touch their body in a sexual way, or attempt or actually have oral, anal, or vaginal intercourse with you?
No___If Yes, enter 1 __

4. Did you often or very often feel that no one in your family loved you or thought you were important or special? Or your family didn't look out for each other, feel close to each other, or support each other?
No___If Yes, enter 1 __

5. Did you often or very often feel that you didn't have enough to eat, had to wear dirty clothes, and had no one to protect you? Or were your parents were too drunk or high to take care of you or take you to the doctor if you needed it? No___If Yes, enter 1 __

6. Were your parents ever separated or divorced?
No___If Yes, enter 1 __

7. Was your mother or stepmother: Often or very often pushed, grabbed, slapped, or had something thrown at her? Or sometimes, often, or very often kicked, bitten, hit with a fist, or hit with something hard? Or ever repeatedly hit over at least a few minutes or threatened with a gun or knife or other life-threatening object? No___If Yes, enter 1 __

8. Did you live with anyone who was a problem drinker or alcoholic, or who used drugs? No___If Yes, enter 1 __

9. Was a household member depressed or mentally ill, or did a household member attempt suicide? No___If Yes, enter 1 __

10. Did a household member go to prison? No___If Yes, enter 1 __

Number of "Yes" answers: _______
This is your ACE Score.

Lack of Protection and/or Nurturing

Sometimes it's what *didn't* happen that causes chronic stress—like being neglected, having an unavailable parent, or a parent who didn't stand up or fight for you, which is what we call "abandonment." My parents were physically around, provided a nice home, material possessions, and an education for us—but they were emotionally unavailable. They didn't provide enough affection, affirmation, and encouragement. We "knew" we were loved, yet we "never felt" loved. Love was conditional, based on "being good."

Add to this that in my mom's generation, being a codependent "submissive" wife was a badge of honor. My mom never modeled assertive behavior, therefore, I let my men control me. Like mom, I learned never to resist my dad—or else be the brunt of his outbursts (control). Hence, I too, became a codependent.

Children are hardwired to respond to a protector. If that doesn't happen, the negative experience can be locked into the brain as a raw, untreated memory—despite the fact the child loved and stood up for parent, and/or was in denial that her needs weren't being met.

Throughout life, we need social contact to regulate our response to distress. In the absence of any close human connections, a person's health cannot be sustained, and depression is common. Merely holding someone's hand, or even looking into a person's empathetic or smiling face can lower blood pressure and levels of stress hormones.[10]

Other Life Stressors

When you took the ACE survey, did you notice there isn't a box to check non-familial things like peer teasing, shaming, bullying, and being excluded or dismissed? I am proof that a targeted child or teen will experience emotional and biological consequences. Siblings, step-siblings, grandparents, aunts and uncles, friends, teachers, coaches and pastors, can also adversely influence a kid and her development.

We've all figured out that "sticks n' stones may break your bones but names will never hurt you" — is a *big lie*. It's more like "sticks n' stones may break your bones but words will break your spirit and heart."

Proverbs 18:21 says life and death are in the power of the tongue — not just a parent's tongue, but any person's tongue. As Scripture bears, *"The words of a talebearer are as wounds, and they go down into the innermost parts of the belly"* (*Proverbs 18:8, KJV*).

Soul Dirt

Why is it that we find it easier to point out someone's failures instead of their fine points? According to Chad Hall, Director of Coaching at Western Seminary, hearing criticism is not only painful in the moment, but it piles up and continues to do harm by keeping us in a stressful state because it's an actual chemical experience in our brain.[11] Social pain activates the same brain circuits that are associated with the brains' processing of physical pain. The experience registers in the part of the brain designed not to reason, but to react.[12]

Rejection and criticism always equal pain. Just as the pain from one criticism begins to heal, a critical person opens the wound back up by firing another painful dart. Each new remark goes right onto the previous pile. It's a fact: We carry around words of criticism and rejection for far longer than we do words of affirmation or encouragement. This is because our *personhood, our soul*, is attacked; compared with "feedback," which addresses our *behavior*. We carry around what I call "soul dirt."

This is what's going on in the brain: Following a painful act, toxic thoughts begin to form tracks which grow deeper and stronger every time we believe that another person has confirmed a particularly strong toxic thought. We then feel *even more* deficient.

Sara's mom constantly tells her she isn't good enough. When her teacher tells her that her homework assignment didn't meet class standards, Sara repeats to herself *again* that she is not good enough, making that toxic thought track deeper and harder to get out of.

For example: A depressed person often perceives others around them as hostile or negative, even when they're not. She may walk into a room and assume everyone dislikes her; she misinterprets innocent looks as "dirty" ones; she mistakes neutral gestures for rejection.[13]

Critical words have a long life and remain toxic long after we think we've disposed of them. This is why we need God's Word, and honest and safe people in our lives—to speak love, truth, and reality. Otherwise, we keep picking up those ugly remarks and ruminate on them unceasingly, and the tracks in the brain only get deeper and harder to get out of.

Pain is Pain

Our immune system can't tell the difference between a critical remark, a rape, recurrent beatings, bullying, neglect, molestation, rejection, teasing and/or shaming. Award winning science journalist, Donna Jackson Nakazawa, stated in her book *Childhood Disrupted*, "It doesn't really matter what the stressor is—poverty, chronic abuse, pressure in school and in sports, or bullying on the bus—stress impacts how the structure and architecture of the brain form. It's a recipe for breaking down the brain."[14]

Many studies link any form of childhood stress, torment, oppression, and persecution to depression and disease in adulthood, as well as a whole vocabulary of NTBs (negative thoughts and beliefs). As adults, theses soul dirt carriers tend to suffer from cardiovascular disease, high blood pressure, obesity, and other mental health disorders.

The good news is—it's never too late! Our brains, at any age, can heal and transform toxic information that has been embedded in our minds for decades. If these key memories are unlocked—identified and treated—then other memories that are associated in the same network will automatically unlock and change as well.

The LORD is the everlasting God, the Creator of all the earth. He never grows weak or weary. No one can measure the depths of his understanding. He gives power to the weak and strength to the powerless. Even youths will become weak and tired, and young men will fall in exhaustion. But those who trust in the LORD will find new strength. They will soar high on wings like eagles. They will run and not grow weary. They will walk and not faint (Isaiah 40:28-31).

Digging into Our Roots

Childhood is a time when we're vulnerable and powerless. Even in the best of childhoods, we may have experiences that are stored as unprocessed emotions and physical sensations. These experiences stay "hot" regardless of how much time elapses.

Unhealed wounds steeped in shame, for example, can trigger behaviors that cause us to hurt ourselves and others. These negative beliefs about ourselves often come from childhood and are of two kinds:

1. *Wounds of omission:* The good things we needed but did not get.
2. *Wounds of commission:* Events that happened that should not happen to any person.

Events such as *parental loss, ongoing parental conflict, economic loss, childhood stress, parental incompetence (ACE risk factors)* have adverse outcomes which are well-documented: deep attachment wounds, low self-esteem, negative self-image, loss of identity, depression and anxiety, poor academic performance, sexual promiscuity, inability to set or respect boundaries, aggressive behaviors, loss of friends, unhealthy and dysfunctional interpersonal relationships, and chemical and behavioral addictions.

I know this sounds depressing, but God's Word gives us hope: *"We are pressed on every side by troubles, but we are not crushed. We are perplexed, but not driven to despair. We are hunted down, but never abandoned by God. We get knocked down, but we are not destroyed" (2 Corinthians 4:8-9).*

Post-Traumatic Stress

Every human being will experience different kinds of stresses and trauma throughout life. Trauma or "Post-Traumatic Stress," is the response to any deeply distressing event that shatters your safe world, so it feels no longer safe. It's what happens when we feel beyond broken.

Often, we find that years after the traumatic experience, something triggers that memory, pushing us to do things to survive the chaos inside. Some turn to drugs or alcohol; others experience depression and anxiety; many act out … and it always affects the family system.

The word for "trauma" means "to wound, damage, or defeat." It is a *normal reaction to an overwhelming event that exceeds our ability to cope at the time.* It's not uncommon for traumatized feelings to increase over time because of an inability to accept the circumstance and failure to process through the painful feelings. "Our brains are wired for connection, but trauma rewires them for protection. That's why healthy relationships are difficult for wounded people", stated Ryan North.

God designed the body's stress system to manage short-term extreme stress—but chronic, enduring stress damages the brain and body. Trauma images may not even surface as a conscious memory, but as *emotions, negative thinking patterns, bodily responses and sensations* long after the event is over. PTSD stands for "Post-Traumatic Stress Disorder."

Post = After | *Traumatic* = Trauma | *Stress* = Anxiety | *Disorder* = Reaction

I'd also say that PTSD stands for *Present Traumatic Stress Disorder* if the person is currently living in an abusive or stress-filled environment. Either way, PTSD is a *deep intrusive injury to the soul.*

I don't particularly like the word "disorder." It implies an illness, disease, or mental problem. I, and many other professionals, believe symptoms stemming from trauma are normal and necessary responses to this kind of personal injury. We call it *Post-Traumatic Stress Injury*—PTSI. In contrast to a "disorder," a stress injury is an emotional wound, able to heal and be transformed.

Whatever your PTSI is, it is unique to you and a natural reaction to the serious injury you sustained.

Big T and Little t Traumas

It is our cumulative exposure, rather than our experience of one specific event, that has the most impact on our overall health. Single-event traumas, particularly in adulthood, seem to process through more quickly because they appear to be more contained in one area of the brain. Multiple and repeated early traumas tend to infiltrate more of the brain, and therefore, are more difficult to resolve.[15]

A big "T" single trauma event may be a life-threatening, time-limited, "single-blow" event such as the sudden death of a loved one, an assault, being robbed at gunpoint, abandonment, a bad car accident (the most *common* cause of PTSD), job loss, terminal illness, terrorism, war, a natural disaster, discovering you've been videotaped having sex and it's all over the Internet, or you've been conned out of all your savings.

If you've been sexually violated, recognize this violation is considered one of the highest factors for the development of PTSD. Symptoms seen in survivors of rape, domestic violence and incest are essentially the same as the symptoms seen in survivors of war. Yet most victims don't recognize they've been through a war; they just think they're defective or crazy.

PTSD may be caused by repeated and/or prolonged events, such as being bullied, criticized, stalked, hit, harassed, yelled at, or rejected. These kinds of small "t" events are not necessarily life threatening but are life-altering because they are a heinous perversion of power, control, and authority. Many people are haunted by events that didn't cause them to feel terror, but rather shame, guilt, anger, or rage.

Some people suffer from a "moral injury" (coined in the late 1990's by a VA Boston psychiatrist). This is when we experience a violation of moral expectations; when our deeply held ethical and moral beliefs are violated. For me it was consenting to have sex with multiple strangers and having an abortion. Those of us who experience a moral injury have similar symptoms to PTSD: emotional numbing, shame, guilt, avoidance, withdrawal, and depression.

Experiencing frequent small "t" events is more harmful than experiencing one big "T" event, say experts.

Daniell Koepke expresses a person's response to trauma,

Your trauma is valid. Even if other people have experienced "worse". Even if someone else who went through the same experience doesn't feel debilitated by it. Even if it could have been avoided. Even if it happened a long time ago. Even if no one knows. Your trauma is real and valid and you deserve a space to talk about it. It isn't desperate or pathetic or attention-seeking. It's self-care. It's inconceivably brave. And regardless of the magnitude of your struggle, you're allowed to take care of yourself by processing and unloading some of the pain you carry. Your pain matters. Your experience matters. And your healing matters. Nothing and no one can take that away.

The impact of any kind of trauma is deeply personal since it is based on *the response* to the event versus the severity of it. So, whatever your stress reaction, know it's how you're wired.

Untreated Memories

A cartoon character sighed, "My brain is like the Bermuda Triangle. Information goes in and then it's never found again."

Sometimes, the memories that our body stores are not always memories we consciously remember. We may have been too young to remember, or we dissociated the experience, or blacked it out—all unconscious choices to detach from reality since our minds tend to repress disturbing information it cannot handle.

Childhood memories can also be misleading because they may simply be images we saw on television or something we heard.[16]

Even the most "functional" families can still leave children with untreated memories. Children are little people without any power. They're very vulnerable Any kind of stressor can feel like death for them.

I can say I had it pretty good growing up. I wasn't neglected, abused, or harmed. For many of us, our symptoms may be due to an accumulation of small t's, like humiliations or being made a fool, that occur at a vulnerable age. Numerous small t's can leave lifelong scars. I developed and carried into adulthood a hoard of negative thoughts, emotions, and physical sensations from my childhood which ran my life—*I'm not smart or good enough. I'm not in control. I feel powerless. I'm always tired.*

For the person who is *not affected* by a particular damaging childhood memory, the event most likely *linked up with other positive memories*. If we had, for example, an experience of being bullied, perhaps an adult told us the bully had a really bad home life, or we just decided bullies are cruel and we weren't going to let them hurt us. We believed, *It's about the bully; not my inadequacies.*

Trinity lived in a very chaotic home filled with drugs, neglect, sexual abuse, and eight other siblings. She had the fortitude to reach out and get help, and receive support from those who did respond with kindness, which allowed her to overcome what many of her siblings could not. The ability to find and connect with nurturing people outside an abusive and chaotic family is a factor frequently linked with resilience.[17]

Today's reactions and behaviors—anger, sorrow, fear, shame, guilt, worry, or anxiety, we assume are tied to a present-day event. In many cases, the reaction is tied to a past memory—because time does not heal all wounds.

Fact: *If a past childhood event had a negative impact, it can certainly be the cause of present-day physical, emotional, relational, and spiritual problems.*

Fact: *Raw untreated memories will continue to generate negative thoughts, beliefs, and feelings when triggered.*

Bad + Good = Better

Fact: *Linking up a bad experience with a good experience can either minimize or negate the experience memory.* This is how we can heal.

Let's say I had been raped as a teenager and today I have a deep-seated fear of most men. Clearly, I also have had other good men experiences such as male teachers, coaches, bosses, and ministry leaders. What can happen is, for example, I can be very loving to my kids one moment, but raging at them the next—all because "some man" triggered my traumatic memory. The two networks—the good experiences about men and this one bad experience—didn't automatically link up.

Freedom can come from targeting the early rape memory that is driving my thinking and reactions today. I can choose to proactively link it up with good and healing information, thereby, restructuring the bad memory into a better and more balanced memory. The essence of The Work is learning how to link past negative memories up with life-giving information, thereby changing the impact of the early original memory on our life today.

† † †

Thankfully, *research supports that many ACE victims manage to thrive.* Many people recover from trauma and grow to be resilient, and become powerful advocates against abuse or do other kinds of wonderful work. Every day you have a chance to change your past and future by reeducating your brain and reprogramming the present.

Therefore, what you have learned, can be unlearned. Lies and false accusations can be un-believed and deactivated when replaced by God's truth. What you *consistently* see and hear over time will enter your heart and mind, and put your life on "autopilot." The key is choosing to get alone and connect with God, immerse yourself in prayer and His Word. Let Him guide you through the counseling and self-examination process. You will begin to see your story line changing.

Visualization Exercise:
Let Jesus Heal Your "Inner Child"

One way to release the past is to acknowledge, listen to, and love the little girl within you. Some of you have been running away from her; others despise her for her weakness and stupidity; and others fear that if her pain comes out will overwhelm and destroy them. This is an important component in the healing process. Work to create a positive memory of Jesus freeing the hurt little girl from the pain which has held her captive for so long.

Close your eyes and visualize yourself as a young girl. You choose the image and her age. *Ask Jesus to help you develop compassion for the young girl who*

endured what you have uncovered. Embrace this hurt little girl and imagine Jesus embracing her with Love.

He says, *"I have never forgotten you despite what you may have thought. I love you (John15:9; 16:27). Did you know I chose you before you were even born (Ephesians 1:4)? You have always been so important and valuable to me. Daughter, you always have had My love, support, and care. I will always be enough for you."*

What does this feel like? Write down your emotional and physical reactions.

Other "Inner Child" Healing Exercises

1— *Talk and connect with this little girl as you would your own child or a student.* You may choose to write her a letter or talk directly to a doll who represents her. Tell her how wonderful she is; that she never deserved to be hurt; that those harmful events don't identify who she is *now*. Express the anger and stand up for her. Tell her she didn't do anything wrong; she wasn't bad, but what was done to her was bad. For example, you can say,

- *You did the best you could. You faced a situation (or situations) no young girl should ever have to endure.*
- *You didn't understand what was happening or being done to you.*
- *You were hurt and suffered, but you survived.*
- *You don't deserve to carry shame and guilt. Those emotions belong to the offender, not you.*
- *You are so lovable.*

Hear Jesus's response, *"I love you. You're not alone. You have me. My grace will be enough and give you the faith to believe and trust (Ephesians 2:8). Together we'll heal the wounds and get through this. I will give you the power and inner strength to do the work. I have great plans for your life (Jeremiah 29:11)."*

2—*Tell the person who hurt her—not literally—"What I want you to know is ..."* Again, you may choose to write the person a letter or speak to a doll.

3— *Finish these sentences:*

- "What is right about me today is ..."
- "I add value to this world by ..."
- "What I celebrate with God about me is ..."

3

Understand the Mind—Body Connection

Woody Allen said, "Life is divided into the horrible and the miserable." What a sad commentary. I think we've all figured out that life isn't a Hallmark movie. There's no guarantee of a happy ever after ending. The thing is, if we want to become aware of what is going on in our minds, we need to look at our life and all the experiences we seem destined to repeat over and over again.

We all have thousands of thoughts we don't know we're thinking. Each thought has a memory and feeling and physiological reaction attached to it. Each one is programmed to generate familiar feelings similar to a past experience. This motivates us to do, or not do, specific things in order to control pleasant or unpleasant outcomes.

To know ourselves is to know how our thinking mind, brain, and body operates together, called *psychophysiology*. There is tremendous value in understanding the mind, brain, and body connection, and how each part connects to adversity and trauma.

Second Corinthians 6:19 states the *"body is the temple of the Holy Spirit, who lives in you and was given to you by God."* It's a pretty important entity. The latter part of the verse reads, *"So glorify God in your body."* One way we can do this is with proper self-care.

Our Thoughts Rule Our Lives

Would you say your thoughts rule your life, maybe they're even killing you? King Solomon wrote, *"For as he thinks within himself, so he is"* (*Proverbs 23:7; NASB*). You've probably heard the saying, "What you think, you become." This happens because human beings process more than 50 experiences per second and have anywhere between 50,000 to 80,000 thoughts per day. That's an average of 2500 to 3500 thoughts per hour! This is because your brain stores *every conclusion* you make about *every experience*. And apparently, 98% of those thoughts are the same thoughts from the day before; and *80% of them are negative and false!*

Judges 21:25 says, "...*everyone did what **they thought** was right*" *(CEV).*

The Brain

The brain is a physical entity and amazingly complex. Brain cells are connected through 100,000 miles of axons that encompass from 100 trillion up to 1 quadrillion synaptic connections. Consider that the Milky Way is made up of only 100 to 400 billion stars.[18] The brain is a vast universe in of itself. There's a lot going on. We only see a small part of it. It's like when we look at the surface of the ocean and we may see some fish and coral and turtles, but we don't see most of the massive ocean that exists.

As the Bible states, we are indeed fearfully and wonderfully made! (Psalm 139:14). Touch the back of your head and neck to feel where your *brain stem* is. This is where you live and breathe.

The brain continually scans itself. Scientists believe the brain processes the capacity to observe the body down to the cellular, even molecular level. For example, our immune system, which identifies and corrects anomalies in the body systems.[19]

As amazing as the brain is, it makes decisions based on biased and convoluted input if that's all we feed it. The more we input negative or fear-based thoughts, the more brain synapses get strung together to generate negative scenarios. Hence, we continually use untruths and half-truths to process our experiences and feelings.

The Mind

The encyclopedia states the *mind* refers to a person's intellect and consciousness as manifested through thoughts, perceptions, memories, emotions, will, and imagination. Theologian Gregory "the Great" (AD 361) believed the image of God is found in our mind. Unlike the brain, you can't see it or touch it. It encompasses all of *the brain's* conscious processes.[20] Our actions come from the proclivities of the mind.

The other thing about the mind is it only has access to what it has learned. It can't use what it doesn't know. If you are given only misinformation and lies, then that's all your mind has access to. If you don't know God's Word, then you don't have access to its power. Jesus said, *"**You are in error** because you do not know the Scriptures or the power of God"* (Matthew 22:29).

The Subconscious

Scientists say the mind focuses on things other than what is actually happening in the present moment. This is because every one of us process millions of thoughts each day "down below" called our *subconscious* or *unconscious*. It compares and analyzes all incoming present-day data with everything in the memory—anything we may have (*past tense*) seen, heard, felt, learned, or understood—until it finds a present-day solution.

Each experience we collect in our brains/minds is tagged with a feeling or feelings and is based on how we see and interpret the experience, called *perception*—and becomes a *memory*. It's always attached to the same feelings we felt when the experience first occurred, at whatever age we were. This is why 35-year-old Janet reexperiences her 5-year-old feelings of fear and helplessness when she thinks about or sees her grandpa, who molested her each time he bathed her when she was five. This is all going on in the subconscious.

Unique Perspectives

One day on a subway train, a woman stood up, slapped the face of the man next to her, and then ran to the exit. Each of the passengers who saw what happened reacted in a personal way. A middle-aged man felt sadness for the man who was slapped. A younger woman was frightened. A teenage boy was stirred up. Another woman felt excitement.

How could the same event trigger such a range of varying emotions? The answer is in our mind's unconscious belief system.

- The sad middle-aged man thought, "He'll never get her back."
- The fearful woman thought, "She's going to really pay for that."
- The stirred-up teenager thought, "She humiliated him; like most women, she must be a real jerk."
- The excited woman thought, "Serves him right. She's strong!"

In each person's case, this event was interpreted, judged, and labeled instantly. The person's unique belief resulted in a different, distinctive, and personal experience of "truth" (which is why so many eye witness accounts are wrong). Think about this: If a little girl has never seen a goat; never seen a picture or had one described to her, and you show her a cow and tell her it is a goat, she'll believe you.

The mind is powerful and easy to manipulate and deceive. That is what the advertising industry banks on … and why Satan targets our minds. William Hazlitt said, "Life is the art of being well-deceived."

Experts say the inclination for self-delusion appears to be weaved into our genetic codes. The biggest person who gets away with deceiving us is ourselves. Have you noticed that we simply believe that our judgment is better than the other guy's? We want to believe we have control over our lives, and self-delusion is usually required.

This is what Jesus meant when He said, *"For they look, but they don't really see. They hear, but they don't really listen or understand"* (Matthew 13:13).

The Mind and Feelings Connection

Since the mind is powerful and easy to manipulate and deceive, so are our emotions. Have you noticed people always *feel* their reality is true? Human beings see and feel everything in their world through their personal "colored lenses" which creates and shapes their perceptions and beliefs, which influences how they feel, and what they say and do in the present. Thus, we create a future like our past.

Feelings arise as a reaction or a response (an internal sensation triggered by the central nervous system) resulting from either a physical or mental experience, or a perception of something on the outside. Feelings are extremely unique and personal.

Scenario #1: When we have a new experience—positive or negative—our brains automatically take a snapshot of what we see (*new experience*), then it finds the *old experience images* in the mind that *match the new present experience*. The closer the new experience connects to an old existing image, the more we will see the new experience in the same light. The new experience links to an old experience like puzzle pieces.

If the old existing image was displeasing, the new image will be displeasing. For example, Robyn's parents constantly fought "ugly" in front of her (*old image*). Today when Robyn hears *anyone* raise their voice in conflict (*new image*), she gets anxious and fearful. Robyn's brain will automatically connect a present-day experience to some specific memories in her childhood of her parents fighting.

Example: I asked my friend what she thought of the new pastor. I hadn't met him yet, but I'd heard several good sermons. Each sermon created a positive memory. Then she began spilling out a negative encounter she had with him. I then created a new memory which attached to my earlier memories of him. My impression of him changed, thereby *revising my earlier memories*. From that point on, every time I saw him, my mind would think he wasn't such a great pastor after all.

Scenario #2: If other things are whirling around in your mind at the same time that you retrieve a particular memory—and if those whirling around thoughts are strongly pleasant or unpleasant, then the brain automatically puts them together like two puzzle pieces.

When this memory leaves the conscious, it is stored along with those other associations. The next time the memory is activated, *it will tend to bring those associations with it*.

Example: Away at college, Tanya had a sneaking suspicion her high-school sweet-heart of four years, Luke, was cheating on her. When she confronted him, he denied it. Yet her gut told her that Luke was lying. When she came home for a visit, while riding the bus, she spotted Luke with "her." Tanya immediately felt nauseous and got off the bus, then promptly vomited in the street. Unbeknownst to her, her unconscious connected the negative feelings about Luke to the bus experience. Tanya, now 30-years old, continues to struggle with a fear of getting on buses.

Example: Britney went to a fraternity party and drank some punch laced with LSD. She began to feel ill and went back to her dorm room where she proceeded to "trip out." All night long she was plagued with hallucinations and feeling completely out of control.

A few days later she was driving to class when a car crossed over the center line, coming straight at her. Luckily, the driver quickly swerved back into his lane. Although there was no crash, the incident triggered the same feeling of being out of control that she'd had in her dorm room tripping out. The memory of feeling out of control linked up to the driving experience. From that day on she had a fear of driving and didn't feel safe in any automobile.

This is also why if you have a cheeseburger, then all of a sudden get sick from the flu, you can't stand the thought or smell of a cheeseburger for a long time, or ever.

Our takeaway: Neuropsychologists state that when two things are held in the mind at the same time, they start to connect with each other.

If we repeatedly bring to our minds negative feelings and thoughts while a particular memory is active, then that memory will be saved and focused in a negative direction, like changing my opinion of the pastor. And since our bodies believe every word stored in our minds, we can also experience toxic physical symptoms and sensations.

The Mind—Brain—Body Connection

The saying "It's *all* in the mind," has truth to it. Our mind and body are one inseparable unit. The *limbic system*, located in the mid-brain, is the mind—body connection; the connection between the psyche (thought) and the physical (the body).

For example, when we're upset in our mind we get "butterflies in our stomach," even physically ill. We don't merely experience anger in our minds, we feel it biologically in our body—our muscles tense, we get red in the face (blood pressure increases), and our stomach aches.

"The interaction between the generally reasonable, rational, ethical, moral conscious mind and the repressed feelings of emotional pain, hurt, sadness, and anger characteristic of the unconscious mind appears to be the basis for mind-body disorders," said Dr. John E. Sarno, author of *The Divided Mind.*

Fact: *What's in the body is in the brain; what's in the brain is in the body.* Dr. Sarno also stated, "The failure of medicine's practitioners to recognize and appropriately treat mind-body disorders has produced public health and economic problems of major proportions in America."

Perhaps this is because physical and emotional experiences can be indistinguishable. Since our nervous system encompasses both brain and body, everything we feel in our bodies is felt in the brain. We literally feel emotional pain and trauma in our nervous system.

The body truly speaks its mind, *"A heart at peace gives life to the body, but envy rots the bones"* (Proverbs 14:30). You may be familiar with the term "psychosomatic" which refers to the effect of the mind, the "psyche," on the body, the "soma." There are a wide range of conditions that people believe are purely physical, such as headaches, but which might actually be brought on by the psyche, such as untreated memories.

No doubt you've heard of the placebo effect. It is a counterfeit treatment which produces powerful positive results in the body's chemistry due to the effect of suggestion. It highlights the strong relationship between mind and body. It has an evil twin called the *nocebo effect* which refers to the power of *negative* suggestion that can lead to bad health, toxic thinking, even 'death by hypochondria.'

Also consider that with adverse experiences and trauma, particularly sexual abuse, the mind finds a way to numb or control the body. The less the body is experienced as a living entity and more an object, the easier it is to function each day. This is what I did to my body and mind through the act of bulimia and incessant dieting.

Mind Your Body

When we experience stress—anything from mild discomfort to intense sorrow, shame, rage, anxiety, or despair—*there is a specific thought causing our reaction, whether we're conscious of it or not.* We also know there is a direct correlation between negative thinking and illness such as cancer, diabetes, allergies, to name a few.[21] It has been estimated that *70 to 90% of all doctor's office visits are stress related.*[22] There is a lot of research showing that mental stress affects our cardiac, respiratory, and immune systems.

What happens is: Thoughts connected to a painful or stressful experience (*a memory*) release negative chemicals that travel through the body changing the shape of the receptors on cells lining our hearts; thereby increasing susceptibility to illness. Toxic experiences cause brain cells to shrivel and die, compared to positive experiences which make brain cells expand.[23]

Numerous studies state that people who focus on negative aspects of themselves, or of life, and consistently believe lies and live by NTBs—for example, "I'm a loser and no one could ever love me," or lies about God, such as, "He is a tyrant and doesn't care about me," they generate waves of fear which release a flood of destructive neurochemicals into the brain.[24] If we were to look at a brain, we could literally see a dark abscess caused by the stronghold of anger.[25] The same is true for every other negative emotion.

A leading (Christian) psychiatrist, Dr. Timothy Jennings, explains the emotional and biological fallout in his book *The God Shaped Brain*:

- We experience anxiety, stress, and fear (PTSI). →
- The *amygdala* (which processes memory, decision-making, and emotional reactions) fires up continuously. →
- Fear circuits are activated and stress circuits are reactive. →
- Shuts down the higher regions of the brain (*prefrontal cortex*). →
- Releases the hormone *cortisol*. →
- Weakens the immune system, kills brain cells, and causes weight gain. (Trauma also floods the brain with cortisol.)
- Produces chronic inflammation and damage to both the brain, mind, and body. →
- Thus love, brain growth, and healthy thinking decrease.

How can this be reversed? Experts say to *practice love and kindness*! It's the healthiest thing we can do for ourselves and families. *Relational health* is essential to our physical, psychological, and spiritual health. Healthy connections (and making amends where necessary) make better memories and create positive thoughts and beliefs (PTBs).

Ruling Negative Thinking Patterns and Beliefs

We are what we think. It's been said that if you tell a lie long enough it becomes a truth. So, if I believe I cannot do something, the belief makes me incapable of doing it. You and I do what we do in response to what we think, which too often is based on lies and misbeliefs.

If we're living the exact opposite of what we desire, there's a 99% chance it's because we have a ruling negative thought pattern—*a false and/or deceptive thought or belief,* that is operating front and center in our mind. *A ruling thought or belief* is an automatic repetitive idea about oneself or situation that creates a deep tread, or impression, in the brain which is attached to a specific and frequently repeated emotional response.

When we experience an adverse situation or trauma, our beliefs become excessively narrow and black and white. For the abused, oppressed, and violated, the brain is super busy looking for confirmation that the world is a scary and dangerous place, and so are the people in it, which can lead to anxiety and other health issues. For example, *I can't trust anyone! This world is an evil and dangerous place, I'm unlovable.* Other examples are believing that people must like us in order to be valued, or thinking "always" and "never" kinds of thoughts.

These kinds of beliefs are life-limiting and "unnecessary suffering." I believe that's what God would call it too. We often think that in order to change our lives we've got to change our behavior, as in behavior modification. This doesn't usually work because *our belief system must be challenged and reformed.* Transformation occurs as we root out the source (the memory) and then adopt new thinking strategies and ways of reacting that line up with God's Truth.

Addicted to Negative Emotions

Did you know we can be addicted to our emotions? When we think of addiction we often think about chemical or behavioral addictions. But we can be addicted to our emotions—to anger, anxiety, sadness, guilt, worry, grief, fear, or depression. A negative feeling can become so entrenched and habitual that a person cannot live without it. Think of it as an endless obsession with one's sorrows, sufferings, and disappointments

Dr. Ali Binazir said we get addicted "because *pain and negative emotions activate the reward centers* of the brain, causing an unconscious addiction to those negative emotions."[26] In other words, we feel excitement and gratification. Some people are addicted to pain because of the attention they receive. I know others who use it as an excuse for a cleaning crew to come in once a month. *Why get well?*

Mindfulness = Health

Conversely, we can say that *70 to 90% of physical and behavioral healings come from a positive thought life.*[27] Healthy, truth-based thinking today has become an integral aspect of treatment for everything from allergies to liver transplants. When we think positively instead of negatively, our tolerance for pain is higher, our recovery from illness and surgery is quicker, and our blood pressure drops; our bodies release the advantageous hormone *DHEA*, and our brains release positive healthy chemicals.

Just because a thought comes into our heads doesn't mean we have to entertain it. When empowered by the Holy Spirit, we can make good thinking choices which change our lives by healing our minds, brains, and bodies. Mind transformation starts with thinking: *I will work at catching those debilitating thoughts and confronting them, rather than entertaining them.*

As you connect with God and do The Work, you will learn that your mind belongs to you, and through His power, you have authority over what you think, believe, and say. He will guide you to restore balance when your thinking is out of sorts. Conclusion: *Mind your thoughts!*

The Eyes

Jesus declared, *"Your eye is a lamp that provides light for your body. When your eye is good, your whole body is filled with light"* (Matthew 6:22). The eyes and brain are intricately woven together. Signals sent from our eyes are deeply processed in the brain. Every experience creates an image and memory, which is stored in the brain's visual center. When a person experiences anything unpleasant or traumatic, the eyes play an important part in what gets communicated to the brain. There's truth in the lyric, "O be careful little eyes what you see."

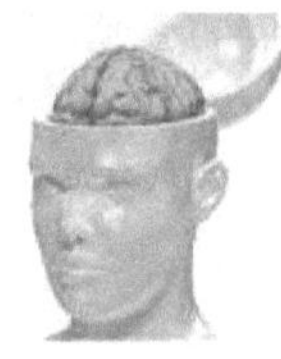

Neurological research states that we can communicate with the brain—and access stored memories—by using the eyes to stimulate a reaction. It has been well-documented that *where you look—where you gaze off to—affects how you feel.* We react differently when we look in different directions. If we look left or right, or up or down, we experience things differently. The difference may be slight or very noticeable.

When you focus on something you have strong feelings about, this recurrent looking left-right or up-down becomes more noticeable. As a counselor, I observe clients doing this repeatedly, even though they're completely unaware they're fixating on a certain spot. (So, don't be automatically offended if someone doesn't look at you straight on when you're talking to them. They're likely processing what you're saying.)

When something important bothers us we become "activated." There are positions in our *visual field* that match up with the places we are holding this distress or "disruption" in our *brain.* Shifting eye position somehow changes what's happening in the brain.[28]

When we locate a "gaze spot," our brain focuses on this position and we are often able to assess where we feel distress in our entire body. We ask: *Does my body feel uncomfortable? Does my breathing change (shorten, quicken, etc.)? What physical sensations arise (i.e., blood pressure rises, get nauseous, hands start to shake, headachy, experience insomnia)? Where are my thoughts taking me?* This is called "brainspotting" in the psychology field[29].

Talk therapy often doesn't get down to the "trauma capsule" of the brain; fixing on a set eye position somehow does.

"If You Can …"

When a crowd brought a demon-possessed boy to Jesus they told Him, *"The spirit often throws him into the fire or into water, trying to kill him. Have mercy on us and help us, **if you can**"* (Mark 9:22). How often do your prayers include the words "If You can …" or something similar?

Jesus responded, *"What do you mean, 'If I can'? **Anything** is possible if a person believes"* (Mark 9:23). "If" thinking only blinds us from seeing Him in all the little things around us. And I believe it limits God from carrying out His perfect plan.

The next verse says, *"The father instantly cried out, "I do believe, **but** help me overcome my unbelief!"* (Mark 9:24) James 1:6 tells us, *"Ask boldly, believingly, **without a second thought**."* (MSG).

In faith, take one more step toward Jesus — this is faith. Hang on to the hope that God specializes in impossible situations. Remember, He created your mind, brain, and body, and *"is able to do immeasurably more than all we ask or imagine, according to his power that is at work within us"* (Ephesians 3:20).

With God the word *impossible* turns into **In-hiM-Possible.**

I love what Julius Richter wrote, "The burden of suffering seems to be a tombstone hung around our necks. Yet in reality it is simply the weight necessary to hold the diver down while he is searching for pearls."

See each struggle as an opportunity for growth. Romans 8:37 promises, *"Despite all these things, overwhelming victory is ours through Christ, who loved us."*

4

The Memory Zone

When you became a Christian, God miraculously brought you out of the world's darkness and into His kingdom of light. He deleted your file marked "sins," but there was no delete key for the files in your memory bank. Since your natural life is not obliterated, everything stored in your mind is still in there, written on your brain's hard drive.

Think of memories as millions of recorded video-clips, basically a blueprint of our lives. Can you remember what happened when you were 1-years-old? The fact is, we all do! However, these memories aren't in our conscious, yet they are foundational. They program our genes and brains to face a particular type of world, and they calibrate how we will respond in relationships.[30]

Every day of our lives, we make more deposits in our memory banks. They affect us, our dream world, and write the scripts of self-talk. They come out of personal experiences and messages from our culture. Ugo Ez said it well, "Be careful who you make memories with. Those things can last a lifetime."

Consider this: Scientists believe because women have a fairly larger *hippocampus* (the part of the brain that regulates emotion, memory, motivation, and learning), they have better memories of the details of both pleasant and unpleasant emotional experiences[31] ... which may be a blessing or a curse. My husband is astounded that I still remember—in detail—what he wore on our first date over 30 years ago.

Every experience and every trauma you've experienced has created an image (*a memory*) which is stored in your brain's visual center. Those images, and all the sensory data from those experiences, can arise anytime if they haven't been adequately processed.

As we learned in the last chapter, new experiences can connect with older existing experiences. For example, if as a young child you experienced a depressed, absent, or alcoholic parent whose moods couldn't be trusted awaiting you when you got home from school each day, then as an adult you might experience dread each day on your way home from work, and not understand that your sense of anxiety is connected to those parental experiences.

Do you have a Facebook account? If you do then you're familiar with the "Memories" feature. If the memory post that pops up for that day is a pleasant one, it's not a big deal. But if the memory post is of your vacation with your ex, it can be the trigger to all sorts of unpleasant side effects — and nightmares.

If a particular negative memory is activated, we can get flooded and blindsided with emotional and physical responses. Ignoring them doesn't work because each time the memory is called up, the neurological pathway strengthens, making it stronger.[32] If this happens repeatedly and we don't take the necessary steps to transform them, recovering from anxious and trauma memories can be difficult, if not impossible.

Your Memory Owns You

Your memory is a monster; you forget but it doesn't. It simply files things away. It keeps things for you, or hides things from you—and summons them to your recall with a will of its own. You think you own a memory; but it owns you!

— John Irving, A Prayer for Owen Meany

Like an elephant, that entity called "memory" never forgets. Did you know that when a mom runs to soothe her crying baby, she is actually tapping into a set of memories from her own early childhood? If her mom cared for her in a loving way, her brain made associations between her own mother's touch, gaze, smile, and other characteristics and pleasure. So now, decades later, when mom attends to her own child, triggered earlier memories causes a release of several important neurotransmitters that are linked with pleasure and empathy.[33] Memories run our lives!

Technically, memory is the ability to take in information, encode it as an image, store it, and then recall and retrieve it at a later time, called *remembering*.

We all store memories in two ways:

1. *Explicit memory*: Is a recollection of specific *detailed* events.
2. *Implicit memory*: Is the *emotional* sense of how the event made us feel; our gut responses.

Many of us who've had a disturbing experience carry forward *implicit memories* of that experience even if we don't exactly remember what happened—*no explicit memory*. These emotional memories have a draw on us all our lives, often unconsciously via those ruling thinking patterns and beliefs. They structure today's thought life. This is because the part of the brain concerned with instinct and emotion (*limbic system*) doesn't have a memory and doesn't know the difference between yesterday and 30-years ago, which explains why some of our childhood experiences are so powerful today.

Trauma and adversity disconnect the left and right sides of the brain. This is why we may have vivid, graphic thoughts about the event, but no emotion. Or, why we experience intense emotions without an actual thought or memory—*no implicit memory*. What is interesting is that when our brain is in this mode it's not focusing on making new memories—unless those memories will be lifesaving.

Memory Processing

Someone said, "Nothing in this world can torment you as much as your own thoughts." It is the mind's job to believe whatever it has stored. *Fact: Most of us are living a lie we were told about ourselves.* Behind every anxious and uncomfortable feeling, there's a thought that isn't true for us, and there's a memory that needs to be treated.

Every memory creates a belief and thinking pattern that desires to run our life. Distressful and harmful memories produce distorted *negative thinking and beliefs (NTBs)* which can be hard to identify. Think of those memories as *untreated wounds* which need to be treated. Therapists use the term "process" to describe the work involved in order to set a memory free.

Treatment = Processing the memory = Healing and Changing NTBs

One of The Work goals is to unlock certain memories and their NTBs that are keeping us stuck. The goal *is not to bring back painful memories and relive the anguish.* We want to connect the present to the past, and look at these events; from a place of compassion, truth, not fear and stress.

To "process" means:

- To address and acknowledge.
- To treat; to convert.
- To move forward; taking continuous steps of action.

Cultural Memories

No matter how beautiful, talented, artistic, or intelligent a woman is, if she breathes, she struggles with insecurity. Insecurities drive us to become something else rather than embrace who God created us to be. We can thank cultural influences which create negative and toxic images and memories. (What the Bible describes as "the world.")

Every magazine we read, every movie we see, each social media view and contact creates an image, and thus a memory. Cultural images either create or reinforce a negative opinion we have of ourselves—and taint other beliefs we have (like political, spiritual, etc.).

For example, in some cultures being overweight is a symbol of beauty. Not in the West. Our view on beauty is the thinner the better; the younger the better. Every time I see a thin young model, I'm made to feel old and dumpy—based on cultural stored memories. I eventually figured out those was no deep hidden memory lurking in my subconscious that has caused me to buy into the be-youthful anti-aging industry so heavily. *Who made fun of me? Who rejected me for my age? What messages did I buy into?* I searched and couldn't find a specific experiential memory. (I do recall my dad condemned "fat" people.)

Conclusion: Decades of listening to and observing this culture's characterization of being good enough, of success and beauty, had created millions of vanity images and memories that *today* drive me to think of myself the way I do, and do the things I do.

Revised Memories

Memories actually get revised all our lives. Our brains continually update, revise, and rewrite certain details based on new input and information, and then erase other details. When we remember an event, the brain replays the tape, imitating the brain's perception of the event. These replays are *not always identical to the original*, but get mixed with present-day beliefs and perceptions. New information and suggestions may become incorporated into old memories. We could say they become clouded, even questionable.

Marlie recalled in 7th grade being grounded in her bedroom all day, on a Saturday, after mouthing off to her mom. She remembers spending endless hours in her room alone, bored and sorrowful. That's her memory. Then her sister tells her that they both got grounded, and their dad made them read the Book of John. Marlie didn't remember that piece of information, but she added it to her memory, thereby revising and changing it.

This means each time we remember an adverse experience, that memory becomes susceptible to changes in how we remember what happened. This is why we want to investigate whether our thoughts are really true.

False Memories

Remembrance of things past is not necessarily the remembrance of things as they were. –Marcel Proust

Did you know we can believe something about ourselves or another situation, when it actually never happened to us? **Not all memories are 100% true.** As children, it is not uncommon to hear a story and take it on as our own.

Example: When Fiona was 10-years-old, her 16-year-old sister Jane, graphically described to Fiona a time when an older boy forced her to touch himself. When Fiona got married, she found she didn't have sexual feelings for her husband. In fact, even as an adolescent, kissing boys never "revved her up" and only made her anxious. This puzzled her because her friends experienced the opposite. She truly wanted to experience intimacy. Fiona loved her husband immensely. Then she recalled a childhood memory. When she was 10-years-old she was forced to touch an older boy's private parts, which repulsed her. Yet, this actually never happened to Fiona; it was Jane's experience. This is always a worthwhile avenue to consider when we begin to explore our beliefs about our past.

We may also unconsciously alter a memory to protect a relationship or person we love. Example: Paula loved her older sister Leah. One autumn day Leah pushed her off a dock into a very cold lake. Leah thought her actions were hysterically funny. Eventually she pulled Paula back up onto the dock. Instead of being angry she thanked Leah for saving her. As an adult, Paula tells a different story. She claims she fell off the dock herself. She remembers how terrified and cold the water was. The day came when God showed Paula this was a false memory. Her subconscious released the true details. Physiologically, she felt better too.

Consider this: It is not uncommon for an offender to blatantly, and *convincingly*, lie and deny they did a horrid offense, thereby rewriting and changing our stored memory of the event. As always, we must pray deeply about our memories.

Trauma Capsules

Memories are bullets. Some whiz by and only spook you. Others tear you open and leave you in pieces. –Richard Kadrey

An overwhelming or upsetting event, can overpower the brain which prevents the information processing system from making the connections it needs to resolve the event. With a normal experience, the brain processes an experience and turns it into a memory.

Contrarily, with a traumatic event the brain can't process it correctly. *Instead, the upsetting memory becomes stored in the brain just as we experienced it,* called a "trauma capsule." Memory capsules are created at the time of a life-threatening event when the mind is so scared that it's going to be harmed or die that everything happening at the moment is locked into the subconscious.

Think of a trauma capsule like a "time capsule"—it contains everything connected to the event: sights, sounds, feelings, touch, and smells that are experienced at the time of the event. These memories are alive and become stuck in time—all the images and emotions, the physical sensations, and the NTBs. They become a raw untreated memory *because they quite often are linking into other untreated memories from the past.* This means that at any time in the future (even 50 years from the event) the trauma capsule can cause panic attacks and re-experiencing symptoms.

Dissociation

Perhaps you're thinking, "I don't have any early memories." This happens quite frequently. Under fight or flight conditions, the brain wants to protect us from further devastation so it isolates the memories of the event so they're no longer connected with the brain's conscious processing of the experience.

One way the traumatized brain reacts is called "dissociation," also referred to as "splitting." It's a mechanism in the brain that allows the person to disconnect from the event, both psychologically and physically. It is a circuit breaker for a nervous system that has become overwhelmed. Think of it as a deeply unconscious survival (coping) mechanism that is triggered in the face of an overwhelming experience. It's the brain's way of preventing PTSD. I think of it as God's mercy.

Lilly is frequently raped by her dad at night. When she hears the door knob turn and the creaking of the door opening at that particular time, she goes into an anxious trauma state. She becomes fearful, agitated, and jittery. When Dad tells her, "Don't tell anyone *or else* ..." disassociating works well in keeping the secret ... until she hears the click of the doorknob the next night. Then the panic attack erupts.

Marielle's husband demanded sadomasochistic acts. To cope with the pain and shame, she dissociates each time. *Numbing* and *avoidance* are closely related. "Avoidance" is the mind's unwillingness to experience unpleasant emotions, thoughts, body sensations, and memories.

"Numbing" is the inability to experience positive feelings; feeling distant from other people, and losing interest in important activities.[34]

Freezing

Dianna's grandfather raped her at 12-years-old. Today, this past event raises in this 28-year-old woman, *a present-day threat of violation* by her closest, most caring friend—her husband. Dianna stiffens, retracts, and collapses in revulsion when she's cuddled by her husband.

Being cuddled and loved by her husband brings up all the emotions attached to her rape. She is reacting to the combined triggers of men and touch. When this happens, in her mind she is confused between a safe and a dangerous person. When her husband gets intimate, *her body and mind go into a survival-based mode assuming danger, even when there is no danger.* Her brain goes into the fight, flight, and freeze mode. In Dianna's case, she freezes. When the lovemaking is over, she immediately leaves the room.

What's going on with Dianna? A trusted adult violated his position of responsibility by sexually victimizing a child. Dianna learned to mistrust any caring advances; fearful they'd lead to further victimization. Her brain installed the event which was interpreted that sex is dirty, painful, and dangerous. These untreated memories became the foundation for a whole host of NTBs and other problems for Dianna.

Sadly, a precious child of God who should have been experiencing intimacy and ecstasy with her husband had been robotically reduced to freeze. As I said before, *when two things are held in the mind at the same time, they start to connect with each other.* This is why we say time doesn't heal all wounds.

BASK Model

The BASK Model can help us put together what is happening in the unconscious memories network. BASK is the acronym for:

- Behavior
- Affect (emotions)
- Sensation (physical)
- Knowledge

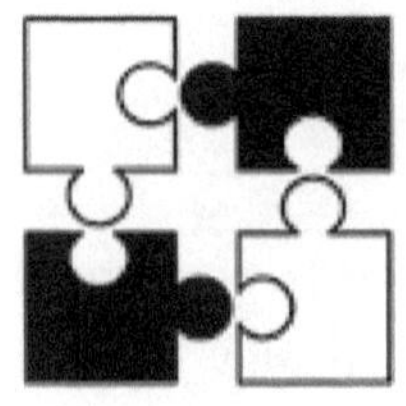 When a memory is processed and integrated, all four components are "puzzle pieced" together. With an untreated memory, the four pieces do not integrate and NTBs tend to run rampant.

Behavior

- Behavior is detached from the other aspects of memory. →
- We think, then act a certain way without knowing why.
  Examples: avoiding intimate relationships, ruminating, vomiting after sex, or the dislike of particular foods or scents.

Affect (Emotions)

- Affect is dissociated from other aspects of memory. There are no feelings attached to the memory. →
  Example: Mandie talks about being raped as though discussing today's weather forecast in a flat affect, matter-of-fact monotone voice.
- Or, we have no memory as to why we feel fear or terror or panic or anxiety.

Sensation (Body)

- Our past can tick away inside us for decades like a silent time bomb — until it sets off a cellular alarm that lets us know our body hasn't forgotten the past. →
- We experience "body memories," psychosomatic symptoms, and/or biological diseases.

Knowledge (Cognition)

- We have full or partial knowledge of a traumatic event.
  Example: We may bring up the experience and say "I remember," yet, the knowledge of the event is disconnected from our behavior, emotions and body language. A person might wonder after watching our reaction if we really did remember the distressing event because we didn't flinch or make a face.

Post-Adverse Growth (PAG)

By now you probably recognize there's a lot going on in your subconscious, which explains why you often have no idea what's running your life story. The good news is we can create positive meaning from our pain, called *post-traumatic growth*, or what I like to call it, *post-adverse growth (PAG)*.

PAG refers to positive life changes in the wake of a traumatic or highly challenging event. Both the Bible and science is clear that people can and do transform negative predicaments, trauma and loss into personal growth and meaningfulness—a "new normal." Tragedies and trauma are not meant to be the last word.

God can turn into good what was meant for evil (Genesis 50:20). This occurs when we bring in new, positive, and truthful information and link it to an old anxious memory. Wendell Berry said it well, "We may strive, with good reason, to escape our past, or to escape what's bad in it, but *we will escape it only by adding something better to it.*"

Each time you add positive and useful information into a negative and painful state of mind, *over time*, the accumulation of positive material will literally change your brain. Your incredible brain rewires itself by focusing attention on a new experience and encoding that image into its neural circuitry. This is why Bible studies, prayer, reading and learning, healing and support groups, and counseling can be very valuable and effective.

For example, pairing a memory of feeling connected to a safe and trustworthy person with an old memory of being abandoned, can enable us to thrive in future challenges. There are great benefits to talking about a painful experience with God and/or another person. "Getting it out" or "fessing up" can buffer the effects of stress. Putting feelings into words diminishes the response in the *amygdala,* the part of the brain that handles fear, panic, and other strong emotions.

Louis Godbold, executive director at ECHO, said, "Trauma recovery doesn't come from a specific tool, but from countless interactions with trustworthy, calm, and loving supportive human beings." The stress response system is built to be calmed by social contact. I tend to feel calmer, better, and less fearful when I can safely express my emotions.

One day Simone had enough of her 3-year-old's tantrum in the grocery store. She snapped and then yelled at the top of her lungs, "Shut-up you little brat!" Those in the immediate area turned to look in horror. Then a huge wave of guilt and shame rolled over Simone. For days she told herself, "I am a bad mother; a bad, bad person." She couldn't get the image of those people's reactions out of her conscious mind. She shared her experience at her weekly mom's group meeting. The women affirmed her and shared their own personal stories of "losing it."

Simone tied this new experience — the new mom's group memory — to the old memory, which changed the direction of her thinking, called "reframing." *Reframe* means to think a different way about a belief, behavior, or experience; to see things from a different angle and redesigning a mindset, in way that sustains and supports healthy changes.She gave herself a huge dose of grace, and changed the trajectory of her belief to "I'm really not such a bad mother."

Although we can't undo or erase a memory, we can weaken its impact significantly[35] by creating positive thoughts and beliefs (PTBs). (Professional counseling may be required.) And …we consciously begin to create new good memories that build hope and anticipation.

Consider memories as building blocks. Instead of collecting the bad memories and using them to build a mental wall to protect us from the pain, we want to start creating good memories. When we build our mind with good memories, we don't build a wall — we build relationships.

✝ ✝ ✝

Peter A. Levine said, "The paradox of trauma is that it has both the power to transform and resurrect." You can experience a *"peace that surpasses all understanding"* and a zeal for life." Yet, PAG doesn't automatically occur as a direct result of adversity. Rather, it's our "constitution" and struggle with the new reality in the aftermath of stress and adversity that determines whether PAG will occur or not. Women every day choose to say no to their present being infected by their past.

Think Straight

One of my earliest memories goes back to kindergarten. My parents were away on a trip and left us kids with a babysitter. For some unknown reason, I chose to not wear underpants to school. In those days little girls wore dresses. My teacher got an eyeful and shamed me for not wearing my panties. In this case it was, *I see London, I see France, I don't see Kimberly's underpants!*

I believe I felt that since Mom and Dad were gone, I didn't have to follow the rules. I felt in control and powerful, something this little girl felt she lacked at home.

As we move from infancy onward, we soak up like crazy what we see, hear and are told by our family, peers, teachers, and mass media, molding our belief system which becomes a pattern of familiarity which is in the background of our adult lives all the time, operating in our minds behind the scenes, like the "great and powerful wizard of Oz" (before he was exposed).

The Massive Brain Root System

Life is like a tree, and our belief system is the massive root structure. Whatever our circumstances, we see everything that's going on through our personal "tree root." Growing up, we accept what we're taught without questioning. The rational, logical left brain convinces us that our thoughts, beliefs, and memories are true. We then rely on feelings generated from these beliefs, which are often false. If it *feels* right, it must be right. This is our emotional right brain at work. It's our default setting. It doesn't tell us that *feelings can lie!* No wonder the Bible warns us, *"Do not be deceived"* (Galatians 6:7).

Sadly, for most of us our tree roots are based on falsehoods. And nothing is going to change *until* a force—God—"re-roots" our lives and frees our minds from untruths.

Your Filing Cabinet of Core Beliefs

To understand how core beliefs develop, create a picture in your mind of a librarian. Give her a "bookish" name.

My librarian is Eleanor. Her job is to file every thought, feeling, belief, and experience that I've ever had into the filing cabinet of my mind. She's got two primary files: "Good experiences and good thoughts/beliefs" and "Bad experiences and bad thoughts/beliefs." The cabinet also contains stories I've heard, or stories I made up in reaction to an experience. Some files are huge; others are small. These are my memory files.

(The body too is like a huge filing system. Everything good or bad we've ever done; our body has a record of it stored away.)

Eleanor's work began in my mommy's womb. The first files she created for me were in response to what my mother was thinking or feeling. This is an important point because some "stuff" going on in my life today may very well have nothing to do with me. I could still be reacting to thoughts or feelings my mom had prior to my birth.

When Eleanor opens a memory file, all of my past thoughts and feelings associated with a certain present-day experience come rushing to the surface—called *remembering*. I can't blame Eleanor for saving the unpleasant, negative, or traumatic memories. She's simply doing her divinely assigned job—sort, categorize, and store *everything*. (That's the brain's job.)

We call these file cabinets of strong patterns of thoughts and beliefs *core beliefs*. Do you think there is a difference between a thought and a belief? There is a difference. A *thought* is something like, "(I think) I'll go shopping because it will make me feel better," or "(I think) I'll stay home where I feel safer."

A *belief* is more set-in stone; more black-and-white. Beliefs are the foundation of our thought life—about God and Christianity, our identity and personhood, relationships, politics, etc. They tend to be *judgments* and are *subjective*; our own personal perceived reality. Beliefs are more significant than thoughts because they make up the core of who we are and run our lives, which is why they're called *core beliefs*.

Core beliefs not only define our behaviors, assumptions and expectations, they become the foundation for our understanding of how the world works, along with what we expect from other people. These subconscious beliefs are triggered once we reach adulthood, by situations that are similar to and closely related with these childhood experiences.

The Inner Abuser Files

Everything we think about, experience, and do is a function of what's stored in our mind's memory files. Many of us are carrying around insecurities and negative messages about ourselves and relationships, such as a parent or teacher telling us we weren't very smart or worse. Their words exerted a powerful influence. Even when we become adults, these messages are so ingrained that we don't question them. We become self-critical and our own worst enemies. I call them our *inner abuser*—the unconscious self-critical voice that calls us names today like *incompetent, ugly, fat, stupid, unlovable,* and *worthless*.

Take myself for example. I became aware that in the presence of a strong personality, I'd feel that what I had to say was not important—"fear of man" consumed my mind. I now know this is the same pattern I experienced growing up. It always had to be Dad's way; I had no voice.

To feel you're not important to a parent leaves you feeling "discarded," invaluable, fearful, with a hole in your soul. As I traversed through thought and memory therapy with God, I recognized one strong core belief—*I'm not important.*

What we need to recognize is that if we've been adversely hurt or traumatized in the fight, flight or freeze mode, our brain gets stuck in that frozen state. It keeps replaying the negative messages we heard when the event happened such as, *I'm not lovable or I'm a bad and weak person,* or *I can't trust any adult,* or *I'm not safe.*

Not only do disturbing experiences build NTBs, but NTBs build distressing memories. An NTB upsets the chemical feedback loops in the brain by putting the body in a harmful state. The brain grows heavy with a thick memory that release a toxic load, interfering with overall bodily function.[36] Consequently, there is a direct correlation between toxic thinking and illnesses such as cancer, diabetes, multiple sclerosis, lupus, heart disease, chronic bowel disorders, migraines, depression, allergies and rashes.[37]

Every body remembers!

The "inner abuser" will continue to lower our self-worth and intrude unless we work to get rid of it. It's not easy and it takes time. But God's power can make it possible. Our mission is to stop listening to our NTBs; stop giving them authority and power over our lives. The greatest way to do this is by listening to the voice of Jesus. Jesus said, *"My sheep [my people]* **listen to my voice; I know them,** *and they follow me" (John 10:27).*

What I also learned it Eleanor's files are not who God says I am. And Eleanor has been all too happy to create new, truth-filled files for me—and continues to this day to do so.

Strongholds: Limiting Core Beliefs and NTBs

Like a computer virus, it's not always easy to detect a false, infected, and painful belief in our minds because they're engrained in our memories. They've become an *automatic* part of our thinking process. And Satan takes advantage of how our brains are designed. He is well aware that deeply entrenched negative patterns of thought can be burnt into the mind thought either repetition or a traumatic experience.

Over time, negative core beliefs and bad habits create toxic neurological pathways in our minds through repetition, called "strongholds." The dictionary says a *stronghold* is something that has a strong hold or powerful influence on a person. It is a mindset that is resistant to change. Synonyms are *stranglehold, vice-like iron grip, cancer,* and *infection.* Interesting choice of words!

Interestingly, strongholds are *literally* embedded in our minds and brains. Brain images show that positive core beliefs look like beautiful, lush, and healthy green trees; whereas negative ones look like ugly, mangled, snarling thorn bushes on a brain scan. I believe fear and shame-based beliefs are the most toxic of all NTBs.

Shame comes out of a lie someone told you about yourself—a lie that you were 'less than.' It's our biggest threat to accepting our identity as God's child. Shame is not the same as guilt. Typically, *guilt* is a result of something *we do; shame* is a result of something *done to us* by another person. The difference lies in the way we talk to ourselves. There's a big difference between *I failed* (guilt) and *I'm a failure* (shame.) As children we learn to shame ourselves rather than being ashamed of our behaviors. We associate normal embarrassment with being worthless.

Have you noticed with shame you feel judged but not known?

The most predominant strongholds women struggle with are:

- I'm incompetent; not good enough.
- I'm not lovable or wanted.
- I'm not attractive; not smart.
- I need to do "something" to get approval and love.
- My needs aren't important; it's not safe to express myself.
- I'm all alone; there's no one to support me.
- I'm powerless.

Are you aware of the strong core beliefs you carry? Begin to think about your own history. What events and predominant family dynamics (ACE memories) stand out as possible contributors to your core beliefs?

Cognitive Dissonance

Romans 6:1 asks a rhetorical question: *"Don't you realize that you become the slave of whatever you choose to obey."*

Since core beliefs develop over time, we're oblivious that we put off positive, truth-based information that contradicts our core belief. When we're confronted with an opposite belief, this creates what is called in psychology "cognitive dissonance." This is when a very strong conviction or belief we have is met with what our minds believe is contradictory evidence, which creates feelings of conflict and friction.

Due to cognitive dissonance, our minds tend to *automatically* go in the direction of seeking evidence to support our core beliefs. In other words, the mind cannot easily trust information or signals that contradict its entire history. This is all taking place in the subconscious.

The problem is that our brains only let in information that confirms our beliefs. For example, the belief is: *The trauma happened, therefore, the world is a very bad place.* Contradictory evidence says: *The trauma happened, and there are still a lot of good people in the world.* The result: I won't believe it because it contradicts my experience.

To support our (false and/or deceptive) belief, we will take our belief and find evidence to support it. *I haven't met any good people, therefore, there aren't any good people left. Just look at the news each night!*

Example: I believe I'm unattractive. My trunk full of images and memories support this—but God tells me that I'm beautiful, awesome and wonderfully created (Psalm 139:14; Songs 4:7). This creates *cognitive dissonance.* A truth versus a lie.

To support my belief that I'm ugly all I have to do is look at some women's magazines, then I'm 100% convinced that the models are prettier than me. This automatically reinforces my belief that I'm ugly. Then those uncomfortable and painful feelings (the cognitive dissonance) disappear because in my mind my (false) core belief is confirmed, not God's truth.

The opposite can happen. We may argue against our NTB by trying to prove we don't believe what our mind is telling us. We create a new thought pattern to contradict the shame of the NTB. For example, Janette's belief "I'm not important" presented itself in a narcissistic manner. She acted out with a sense of entitlement, arrogance, and pride. Her mind needed to prove she was important—versus confirm she was not important. It's a different kind of cognitive dissonance.

This battle of the mind reminds me of the devil versus angel cartoon images we've all seen. Jeremiah 17:9 reminds us that the heart is deceitful above all things. *Feelings are not facts.* Our emotions don't always reflect reality and truth. If we simply follow our minds and do what feels right, we will be led astray, which is exactly what the devil desires. This is why we need Jesus's truth and help 24/7.

The Intruders

Unwelcome thoughts and memories are what we call "intrusive." These intruders come at random when triggered. They may emerge as a physical feeling, an image, a strong emotion or a flashback (the sensation of being partially or fully back in the place and time, as if the event were happening all over again.) They are demanding. They hijack our attention and make it hard to concentrate on anything else. There's no end to turning them off—called "rumination."

Ruminate means we reflect on something *repeatedly* in our minds; we over-analyze; worry about a stressful event; we wrestle with the future hoping something positive will emerge, yet, all we do is create a field of thorns and weeds in the mind. Chronic rumination will lay down deeper and deeper tracks of toxic thinking, which in turn run our lives ... and are at the root of depression and anxiety, and many physical issues.

The intruders can also take the form of reenactments or "compulsive re-experiencing" in which we repeat the behaviors of the event (the trauma) or we expose ourselves to information or situations that recall the adverse event.

Popular Ruminating Phrases

Are you one of the many women who ruminate about how you'd have liked things to be different? *If only; What if; I should have; I could have; Never; I can't.* Other words are: *would, ought* and *I wish I; I wish you had; it used to be; it could have been.* These are phrase that pull us back into a past that never really existed.

Thoughts such as, *I should be doing this ... I should be thinking this ... I should be feeling this ...* only accentuate whatever negative view we already have of ourselves. Let me add, if you beat yourself up with a lot of *I should have ...* statements, please tell yourself, "I was doing the best I could at the time."

Win the Battle with Mindfulness

We need to get this: *Much of the stress we feel is usually caused by arguing with something that is NOT today's reality!* What we think or feel about the past, and what it actually has been, are two different things. We've got to focus on where we are—not where we wanted to be, or thought we should be, or wishing something hadn't been. That's not reality. *We need to accept "what is."* Today counts.

Learn to ask yourself this very important question, *How can it be helpful and healthy to argue with or ruminate on something which has already happened, something which may not be my business, or something that hasn't happened?* Answer: It's not helpful.

The battlefield for every believer is in the mind! God understands intruders and how easy it is for us to get lost when we follow ruminating thoughts and beliefs. How we choose to think is essential to living the life Jesus desires we live.

The opposite of rumination is *mindfulness*—focusing and stilling our attention on the present moment; a deliberate openness to connecting to and taking in the presence of God. There are numerous instances in the Bible where we're told to "be still." In Hebrew the word "still" means to *cease striving; to collapse and fall limp.* Meditation exercises can be very helpful. What we're doing is creating a new neural tract in the brain; a new "go to" place for our mind when we start ruminating. Begin to practice being intentionally "still" in Jesus's presence.

Neuroplasticity

It's been said that there's no such thing as a gray sky. The sky is always blue. However, sometimes gray clouds come out and cover up the blue sky. It's like that with our minds.

Gray clouds don't last; blue sky does. We've been designed by God to build good thoughts which lead to a healthy soul, mind, heart, and body. Second Timothy 2:7 tells us as Christians we have a *sound mind;* and 1 Corinthians 2:16 tells us we have the *mind of Christ.* In other words, *you have an amazing divine mind!* It has the power to heal your thought life and body!

According to doctors at the MITA International Brain Center, the brain is equipped to change rapidly and biologically reshape itself.[38] It's called *neuroplasticity. Neuro* = brain cells; *Plastic* = changed and altered.

We have the perfect mind of Christ, yet it gets clouded with fearful patterns and distorted beliefs because the devil and the world are pros at invading our minds with lies, accusations, and confusion. When we start to input the truth about ourselves and specific events which are tied to our thoughts and memories, our brain will begin the process of restructuring itself. *The key is to align ourselves with God and His Word to create an experience, which creates a memory, that deeply communicates truth.*

Finding out how you've been designed and how God feels about you may be the most surprising discovery you'll ever make. It will provide immunity against criticism and rejection. The more we meditate and visualize scriptural truths about ourselves, the more we'll believe them; the more we'll program ourselves for successful change and self-criticism, the more each chain of bondage will break away.

Romans 8:5-7 states, *"For those who live according to the flesh **set their minds** on the things of the flesh, but those who live according to the Spirit **set their minds** on the things of the Spirit. [6] For to **set the mind** on the flesh is death, but to **set the mind** on the Spirit is life and peace"* (ESV).

God gives us the choice to set our minds on the things of the kingdom (Spirit), or the things of this world (flesh and Satan). He also gives us a command, *"… set your mind on things above …"* (Colossians 3:1; ESV). As we do, old beliefs will begin to lose their power and in time fade away.

We can pray Paul's prayer, *"I pray that the perception of my mind may be enlightened …* (Ephesian 1:18; HCSB). God specializes in restoration and redesign—a new life, a new mind, and a new story untainted by any untruths.

✝ ✝ ✝

A friend placed in my hand a book called *True Peace*. It was an old mediaeval message, and it had but one thought: that God was waiting in the depths of my being to talk to me *if I would only get still enough to hear His voice*. I thought this would be a very easy matter, and so began to get still. But I had no sooner commenced than a perfect pandemonium of voices reached my ears, a thousand clamoring notes from without and within, until I could hear nothing but their noise. Some were my own voices, my own questions; some my very prayers. Others were suggestions of the tempter and the voices from the world's turmoil.

In every direction I was pulled and pushed and greeted with noisy acclamations and unspeakable unrest. It seemed necessary for me to listen to some of them and to answer some of them; but God said, *"Be still, and know that I am God."* Then came the conflict of thoughts for tomorrow, and its duties and cares; but God said, *"Be still."*

And as I listened, and slowly learned to obey, and shut my ears to every sound, I found after a while that when the other voices ceased, or I ceased to hear them, there was a still small voice in the depths of my being that began to speak with an inexpressible tenderness, power and comfort.

As I listened, it became to me the voice of prayer, the voice of wisdom, the voice of duty, and I did not need to think so hard, or pray so hard, or trust so hard; but that "still small voice" of the Holy Spirit in my heart was God's prayer in my secret soul, was God's answer to all my questions, was God's life and strength for soul and body, and became the substance of all knowledge, and all prayer and all blessing: for it was the living God Himself as my life, my all.

–Written by *A. B. Simpson,* published in Streams in the Desert (June 30)

Part Two: The Work-Out

Uncover and Restructure Negative Thinking Beliefs and Anxious Memories

My beloved daughter,

You are Mine, and you are called personally by Me. That's why it is hard to watch you hold on to your past. I see you differently than you see yourself. You see what you've done, but I see what I want to do in you. You see where you've been, but I see where I want to take you.

I have you covered, precious one, and I will use every mistake you've made as a tutor to make you wiser. As My daughter, you have the privilege and the choice to live an abundant life filled with joy, adventure, passion, and purpose. Don't hold on to things that hold you back from My blessings. Your past has paved the road that led you to Me. Your past does not have to define you anymore. It is finished.

Now ask Me to do a new thing, to make a way in the wilderness, and to increase your faith in ways you never dreamed possible. Take My hand, and let's walk forward together into your new life.

Love,
Your heavenly Father

Written by Sheri Rose Shepherd, *HisRoyalFamily.com*

6

Techniques to Help You Through *The Work*

Today depression and anxiety are America's "new normal." The pressures and stress some days literally take our breath away. When we're upset and worried, it's hard to try to solve problems, stay focused, and do recovery work. We wonder where the abundant life God promised is found. Therefore, before each Work-out session, we want to reduce stress and tension in the body and mind, and create a focused Christlike mind using a combination of approaches that prompt the relaxation response:

- Deep breathing
- Body relaxation
- Eye movement
- Create a Jesus safe and calm place
- Visualization

How we breathe can give us valuable information. Our breath is closely connected to anxiety. *What is your inhale like: Is it full, tight? What about your exhale?* We can befriend stress, and anxious NTBs and memories, through practicing deep breathing exercises which can help anchor us in the present moment.

Second, learn to pay attention to your body sensations. Recognize that once you start The Work you could experience some shaking and trembling. This is normal. It's the body's way of bringing a person out of trauma and returning their body to a state of groundedness.

If you begin to weep, this is normal. Embrace it. Your soul is beginning the process of grieving and healing. Being conscious of your body sensations can help you to anchor into the present. Explore and notice all that you can about how your body feels.

Never forget that your body is a sacred object. First Corinthians 3:16 asks a rhetorical question, *"Don't you realize you are the temple of God and that the Spirit of God lives in you?"*

*Read through all the techniques first to familiarize yourself with them.

Deep Breathing

"The LORD your God is in your midst ... He will be quiet in His love."

—*Zephaniah 3:17 (NASB)*

Deep breathing (a.k.a. *abdominal breathing; belly breathing*) is when you breathe deeply and intentionally; the air coming in through your nose fully fills your lungs, and the lower belly rises.

Breathing exercises oxygenate the blood and the cells, supporting all life-giving biological pathways and move energy. It is a great way to de-stress and relax deeply and move any stuck feelings in the body or mind. Through *deep abdominal breathing,* we can begin to relax and calm down. Then the reactive part of the brain shifts to the *prefrontal cortex,* which is where clear thinking and wisdom resides; where thoughts and actions are coordinated.

When people are stressed, they tend to breathe shallowly from their chests rather than their stomachs. Deep breathing from our stomach activates a different brain pathway which causes the brain and body to slow and calm down.

Professionals agree that to overcome the unhealthy day-to-day stress response, we should practice this type of breathing daily, regardless if we're feeling stressed. Deep breathing can prevent the stress response from overacting in the first place.

- Find a quiet, comfortable place to sit. Sit up straight.
- First, take *a normal breath* and relax.
- Place both hands on your ribs.
- Breathe in normally. Focus on feeling your ribs rise.
- Breathe out *slowly* through your mouth (or your nose, if that feels more natural) allowing your chest and lower belly to rise as you fill your lungs. Let your abdomen expand fully. Feel your ribs rise.

- *Exhale slowly*—when you exhale, imagine blowing out all your worries, concerns, and fears.
- Now slowly take 3 deep breaths: 1—2—3. Inhale God's strength and sufficiency; inhale His grace and love.
- Repeat several times.

Another popular method is Dr. Andrew Weil's *4—7—8 Breathing*:

- Breathe in for 4-counts, hold for 7-counts, and breathe out for 8-counts—slowly.
- Breathe out slowly through your mouth (or your nose, if that feels more natural).
- Now try breathing in for 4-counts; out for 8-counts—slowly.
- Repeat several times.

You may want to try placing your *hands on your heart*. For some people it is a gentle form of touch or feeling held by a loved one. Remember, every breath means you are still alive and that the most important part of your life is still ahead of you.

Breathe in God

For many of us, we're just trying to survive the day. We forget that when we were formed in our mother's womb, God gave us breath. *"Then the LORD ... breathed the breath of life into the man's nostrils, and the man became a living person"* (Genesis 2:7).

God never intended for us to be constantly off and running, gasping for air. Think of breathing also as a spiritual act of taking in the breath of empowering love, truth, grace, and mercy. I think God whispers, *Stop. Stay. Breathe Me. Only I can give you the life-giving Spirit.*

Allow Him to infuse you with His breath of life. That's all you need to face each day. Pray, *As I breathe in and out today by Your Spirit, I receive Your breath and Your love, truth, grace, and mercy.*

Body Relaxation—Tense and Release

When we try to fight our own battles, we tend to bear the weight in our bodies. Quiet yourself down and slow your breath. Then scan your body with your mind to identify where any tension may have settled. When you find that point, or points, say in your neck and shoulders, do this exercise. Tensing and releasing muscles helps the body relax.

- Sit comfortably or lie on the floor. Close your eyes.
- Flex and tighten your [tense area of body] for 2-seconds while inhaling deeply.
- Hold your breath and then exhale deeply.
- Relax your tightened muscles after each deep exhale.
- Then do this with all your muscle groups starting from your head to your toes.

Eye Movement Exercise

This eye exercise is used to coordinate the hemispheres of the brain to receive and process new material.

Begin with center focus: With your eyes open, hold your head steady and focus on a spot on the wall directly in front of you. Hold each position at least 5 seconds. Observe whether you have any type of eye, facial, or bodily reaction in a particular spot. You may feel a more intense sensation or disturbance emerging from a place in your body when you are focused on a particular eye position. Don't dismiss this.

- **Up.** Stretch your eyes as far up as possible—try to look at the top of your head.
- **Center focus.** Then bring your eyes back to the focus point. Briefly close your eyes and then open them. (Repeat after each movement.)
- **Center right.** Stretch your eyes as far as possible to the right.
- **Center focus.**
- **Center left.** Stretch your eyes as far as possible to the right.
- **Center focus.**
- **Center down.** Stretch your eyes as far down as possible—try to look at your feet or floor.
- **Center focus.**

- **Upper right.** Stretch your eyes up to the right.
- **Center focus.**
- **Lower right.** Now far down to the right.
- **Center focus.**
- **Upper left.** Stretch your eyes up to the left.
- **Center focus.**
- **Lower left.** Now far down to the left.
- **Center focus.**

Create a Safe Jesus Place in Your Mind

As you begin to process the upcoming information and implement the exercises, it is critical to create in your mind a safe and calm place to counter any feelings of anxiety or other upsetting emotion.

Your Jesus Safe Place can be an anchor to help keep you clam and grounded in the present moment. Think of it like "home," a place you can return over and over again to regain balance. When your mind starts ruminating or journeying off into the past, or you begin to feel distress, you can return "home," to your Jesus Safe Place.

> *Jesus was sleeping at the back of the boat with his head on a cushion. The disciples woke him up, shouting, "Teacher, don't you care that we're going to drown?" When Jesus woke up, he rebuked the wind and said to the water, "Silence! Be still!" Suddenly the wind stopped, and there was a great calm.*
>
> *Then he asked them, "Why are you afraid? Do you still have no faith?"*
>
> *The disciples were absolutely terrified. "Who is this man?" they asked each other. "Even the wind and waves obey him!" (Mark 4:35-41)*

If Jesus could calm and rescue the apostles, He's able to rescue us from the storms of everyday life. Jesus *can* calm every storm—every trauma—every triggered memory—every upset gut—every asthma attack—every "train wreck." He is our Healer and safe place (Psalm 46:1).

My (Kimberly) Jesus Safe Place: For years, I had dreams where I'd be trapped in an ocean, surrounded by creatures like whales. They never harmed me but I could never reach the surface of the water. Then I'd wake up. I'd be so relieved it had only been a dream. Now that Jesus is in my life, I no

longer have these dreams. When I came across this image of Jesus, I chose it to be my Jesus safe, calm place (image).

Create Your Own Jesus Safe Place Image

• *Close your eyes and focus on an image of Jesus.* Notice the colors and any other sensory experiences that go with it. What does it feel like? How is your body responding—your chest, stomach, shoulders or face? How is your mind responding?

• *When you focus on this image, where do you feel a calm, grounded feeling in your body the most?* To your left, middle, or right?

• *Add deep breathing.*

• *Find a personal Scripture* to attach to this image; one you can memorize. For example,

✓ "Don't be afraid, for I am with you. Don't be discouraged, for I am your God. I will strengthen you and help you. I will hold you up with my victorious right hand" (Isaiah 41:10).

✓ "Your own ears will hear him. Right behind you a voice will say, "This is the way you should go," whether to the right or to the left" (Isaiah 30:21).

✓ "The LORD says, "I will guide you along the best pathway for your life. I will advise you and watch over you" (Psalm 32:8).

✓ "Trust in the LORD with all your heart; do not depend on your own understanding. Seek his will in all you do, and he will show you which path to take" (Proverbs 3:5-6).

✓ "The LORD is my light and my salvation—whom shall I fear? The LORD is the stronghold of my life—of whom shall I be afraid" (Psalm 27:1)

✓ "LORD, help!" they cried in their trouble, and he saved them from their distress. He sent out his word and healed them, snatching them from the door of death" *(Psalm 107:19-20).*

*Not every technique will be a person's "cup of tea," as they say. If this doesn't work for you there are numerous other ways to lower the stress response and learn to calm ourselves and rest in God. Do your research and ask others what works for them. A Christian meditation app I use is called *Abide*. A speaker guides you to rest and transform your mind by listening to Scripture-based peaceful directed meditations.

EFT (Calming Exercise)

This is called *Emotional Freedom Technique* (EFT), also referred to as tapping or psychological acupressure to increase positive feelings of a safe place.

- Close your eyes. Cross your arms in front of you with your right hand on your left shoulder, and your left hand on your right.
- Then tap your hands alternately on each shoulder 4 to 6 times.
- Bring up from your memory your Jesus safe place.
- Go into a safe and calm place.
- Again, tap your hands alternately on each shoulder 4 to 6 times.
- If the positive state increases, you can use this technique as needed.

Try Yoga

The purpose of yoga is to build strength, awareness and harmony in both the mind and body. Maintaining a regular yoga practice can provide physical and mental health benefits. Health clubs offer it, or you can purchase a DVD and do it in the privacy of your own home.

Treat yourself to a massage!

Massages and touch activate an oxytocin physical response.
(Scientists found that when a person is dealing with "social coldness" like betrayal and rejection, the same neural brain structures are engaged as when the person touches a cold object or feels physically cold.[39] Contrarily, being held close creates both physical and "social warmth" of trust and caring. Is this why so many of us like to meet for a hot cup of coffee—to increase social warmth and closeness?)

Experience the Real Jesus:
A Visualization Exercise

Albert Einstein said, "Imagination is more important than knowledge."

Start by visualizing Jesus in a safe wondrous place. You can see Him far off. He's running towards you because He's been desperately seeking you. Here He comes. He's ecstatic He's found you; the Person who died for you. You move towards Jesus, and step out of your fears, doubts, insecurities and woundedness. You embrace. Look into His face. See His perfect love for you beaming from His eyes. Feel your fears and anxiety dissipate. In a soft-spoken voice hear Him say to you,

My precious daughter, I love you more than you could possibly imagine—beyond anything you can intellectualize or imagine. You may have been hurt and traumatized; your life may be in shambles, and it may not have turned out as you've dreamed. Don't lose hope. My divine power has given you everything you need for a godly life (Peter 1:3). I AM the Great Physician and the Perfect Counselor. The same power that kept me nailed to the cross and brought me out of the grave, is the same power I will use to transform and heal you. My power is available to you right now. What sin has disrupted; the power of my Spirit can restore. No one can snatch you out of my hand (John 10:27-30). Together we're going to conquer the struggles and heal your wounds. You will shine like the sun as you recover and discover the truth. I will accomplish infinitely more than you might ask or think (Eph. 3:20) through the spiritual gifts I've given you (1 Cor. 12:7). I have something great for you (Jere. 29:11). Believe it daughter! I do not lie (Num. 23:19). Say yes to My Love.

It's time to start The Work!

If you feel anxious about moving forward this "Suitcases on a Conveyor Belt" exercise may help you.

Imagine a conveyor belt at the airport loaded with suitcases. Each suitcase represents specific topics and areas and seasons of your life. They are packed full with thoughts, feelings, and memories about those times. We need to take a suitcase off the conveyor belt and unpack it so we can see everything that's there. *However, we don't need to do that for each suitcase that goes by on the conveyor belt.* Pray, asking the Holy Spirit to guide you as to which suitcases need to be grabbed and then opened. You can feel secure He is telling you which one to grab and open.

Overview: Work-Sessions Steps

This is what the LORD says— your Redeemer, the Holy One of Israel: "I am the LORD your God, who teaches you what is good for you and leads you along the paths you should follow. –Isaiah 48:17

Session 1: Locate Your Early Origin Memory in 6-Steps

Step 1—Prepare your mind, brain, and body.

Step 2—Bring up a recent disturbing event.

Step 3— Describe and record your responses regarding this event.

Step 4— Describe the emotional sensations you are feeling.

Step 5— Describe the physical sensations you are feeling.

Step 6— Find a gaze point; Connect this event to a past event.

Session 2: Detect Your Greatest NTBs in 3-Steps

Step 1: Get to Know the NTB categories.

Step 2: Identify Your Primary NTBs.

Step 3: Explain how these NTBs affected you in the past and presently.

Session 3: Change a Negative Thought & Belief in 6-Steps

Step 1—Name your NTB.

Step 2— Establish the EOM and NTB connection.

Step 3— Focus on the NTB. What emotions arise?

Step 4—Describe how your body feels; it's reaction.

Step 5—Question and investigate the truth of the NTB.

Step 6—Create a new PTB; a truthful thinking tract.

Session 4: Update and Renew an EOM in 6-Steps

Step 1—State your EOM as you remember it.

Step 2—How has this memory affected your life in general?

Step 3—How does this EOM make you feel emotionally?

Step 4—When you believe this EOM, how does your body react?

Step 5—Question and investigate the truth of the EOM.

Step 6—Create a revised memory by adding a new positive experience to it.

Remember: *If God wants us to do something, He'll give us His power to do it.*

Begin each day's work by checking in with yourself and asking yourself how you feel in your mind and body, and in the present moment. Read through each technique first. Make your work a conversation with Jesus. Take your time. It's okay to do one step a day or every couple of days. Ideally you will be working with at least one other person who will walk you through each session. Don't try to direct the process. Let the Holy Spirit guide you. Trust Him. He is your gut instinct.

There is no deadline to complete these exercises. Always use prayer and your breathing and relaxation techniques to bring yourself back to your Jesus Safe and Calm place.

Optional Prayer (Personalize as you feel lead)
Father, I see myself and the world through a faulty lens; through my pain. I want to see my life in a new godly way. Help me use these new practices to change my view and perspective; to discard my old lens and put on a brand new made-by-God lens over my mind, brain, and heart. Thank you for the work you are doing in me. In Jesus's name.

Here we go. Let's do The Work!

7

Identify an Early Origin Memory in 6-Steps
(Session 1)

How are you feeling right now about starting The Work? *Reluctant? Fearful? Anxious? Excited? Something else?* This is normal. When I find myself in these kinds of circumstances I'm reminded of the story of Joseph in the book of Genesis. Joseph was the outcast brother who was sold into slavery, forgotten in prison, and accused of rape … but then because of a gift God gave him (interpreting dreams) he finds himself second in command in all of Egypt. His brothers' malicious actions were actually used by God in order to position Joseph to save his biological family.

While Joseph wouldn't have chosen the path his life took, he could look back at the course of his life and see the ever-present hand of God. The things his brothers meant for evil were ultimately under God's authority. Joseph felt compassion for his brothers and wept, *"You intended to harm me, but God intended it all for good. He brought me to this position so I could save the lives of many people"* (Genesis 50:20).

No evil plan of humans can thwart God's purposes. Job, who also endured extreme hardship proclaimed, *"I know that you* [God] *can do all things; no purpose of yours can be thwarted"* (Job 42:2).

We can find hope to face the complex, and often tumultuous, circumstances and memories of life. We have the knowledge of the sovereign God. God is not surprised by all of this; He's not a loss on how to respond and help us heal. His plans can never be defeated. *He will accomplish exactly what He intends in our lives!*

I hope you feel spiritually strengthened to now move on.

Those Nasty Hidden and Unprocessed Memories

Has something like this ever happened to you?

- *Event:* I'm getting dressed in the morning.
- *Thoughts:* My stomach is way too big. I look like I'm pregnant. It's my fault. I've been eating way too much lately. I'm a porker.
- *Emotions*: Shame, depressed, bitter.
- *Action:* Change the outfit; pledge not to eat dinner and workout an extra hour for the next week.

Every woman experiences something comparable. Weight is not the real issue. Most likely there is *a more upsetting belief* that's affecting you. Critical words and traumatic events have a long life and remain toxic long after we think we've disposed of them. Perhaps someone in your past called you "Fatty Patty." Or the opposite—you were praised for being skinny, which became an expectation.

Most people have about 10 to 20 untreated adverse memories that are responsible for most of their NTBs and pain. Once the memories are identified, treated, and stored appropriately, the old disturbing emotions, thoughts and physical sensations can subside. It's like once these old toxic memories are exposed as the "bad guys," then the "good guys"—the positive thoughts and beliefs, can take over.

When you have an upsetting thought or memory, get in the habit of asking yourself what your body and mind's reaction is. If you cringe, go to a negative place in your mind, feel a funky physical sensation, or some other disturbing response, then most likely you haven't adequately processed the event. If your mind and body didn't react in a particularly negative way, you can say your brain processed the event and the memory no longer is a stronghold.

Moving Forward

As I said in the beginning, while we don't have the power to directly obliterate or magically change our thoughts, emotions, and memories, we have the ability to change the image with which our emotions are associated—by *carefully choosing and adding new experiences* that will help create new neural structures and rewire old brain pathways effectively—thereby radically restructuring them and changing our life going forward. This is what The Work is all about.

Our first task is to open our suitcase of untreated memories and to identify the associated negative thoughts and beliefs (NTBs) that are attached to them, and then work to transform them into treated neutral or *positive thoughts and beliefs (PTBs).*

The Work is not going to coach you to relive your past; merely to remember past key events which are keeping you stuck today and living in the land of giant NTBs. These past memories I call *Early Origin Memories (EOMs).* "Origin" means something from which something else arises; the point of derivation or originality.

We want to wisely bring certain EOMs into the present so we can see how they tie to our present-day physical, emotional, biological, relational, and spiritual life—and then transform them.

EOMs will never go away entirely, but as one doctor put it, "The feeling of living in a pressure cooker will abate as the steam is allowed to escape slowly through surfacing memories." This is why it's important to work through anxious memories.

The goal is to *unlock and unblock,* and choose to look with wonder and self-compassion and curiosity—not fear. Someone said, "Knowledge ties the past to the present, but wisdom from God takes the present and moves it to the future." *"For the LORD gives wisdom, and from his mouth come knowledge and understanding"* (Proverbs 2:6).

In this first session you will be coached through 6-steps and asked to write out exactly what comes to your mind when you answer each step question. Writing out certain memories and thoughts can be difficult. Pray and gently push yourself forward. Remember, 20-minute writing sessions about emotional topics, on consecutive days, reduces PTSD symptoms, depression, and anxiety after 2-weeks.[40] Writing has been clinically associated with improved health.[41]

The 6-steps in this session are:

1. Prepare your mind, brain, and body.

2. Bring up a recent disturbing event.
3. Describe and record your responses regarding this event.
4. Describe the emotional sensations you are feeling.
5. Describe the physical sensations you are feeling.
6. Find a gaze point; Connect this event to a past event.

SUD: Subjective Units of Distress

To begin, I'm going to introduce you to the *Subjective Units of Distress* or *SUD scale*. You'll be asked at several points to jot down your SUD number—how distressful and disturbing the event and memory feels, from *0 (no distress)* to *10 (extreme distress)*. If you feel your SUD level is 3 or higher, the memory is likely raw and untreated.

Example: [*Recent event*] Michelle found it difficult to concentrate at work. She expected failure at every turn. She was prone to rants and rages not only at work, but at home which jeopardized both her family and career. Every rant created this belief: "I'm an out of control failure." She rated this belief on the SUD scale a 7.

Sara's early origin memory (EOM) pointed to her mom constantly telling her that she wasn't good enough [*memory 1*]. Then she remembered when her teacher told her that her homework assignments didn't meet class standards. It affirmed to her, *again,* that she is not good enough [*memory 2*]. Memory 1 linked up with memory 2 which made her feel like a complete failure which carried into adulthood. She rated her SUD an 8—deeply distressing.

In this session, we will be using a worksheet like this one:

Event	**SUD**	**EOM (early origin memory)**	**SUD**
Incident			
Emotions			
Body			

Optional Pre-Work Prayer (Personalize as you feel lead)

Dear Father, I declare my dependency on You, for apart from You I cannot do The Work. I need your help. Help me to locate the beliefs and memories that have me stuck. What lies are behind them? Please fill me with Your Holy Spirit and guide me into all truth. Show me what I need to see and give over to You. I ask for Your complete protection and guidance. Thank You for the work you are already doing in me.

In the name of Jesus.

Work-Steps: Locate an EOM in 6-Steps

Step 1—Prepare your mind, brain, and body.

- Find your Jesus safe place; a place where you feel calm and grounded.
- Do some deep breathing until you feel ready and relaxed.
- Listen to your breathing. Don't try to slow or alter it.
- Breathe in God's goodness and love; breathe out any anxiety or fear.
- Do the eye movement exercises on page 73-74.

Step 2—Bring up a recent disturbing event.

Think of a present-day event that currently bothers you; where you feel distressed and disrupted by this issue.

Step 3— Describe and record your responses regarding this event.

- Write a brief description in the event column in the first row marked *Incident,* that describes what happened.

  Example: I told Caroline a secret which *she promised* to hold between only us, yet she told her husband.
- Give it a SUD number. Caroline's SUD is 7.

Event	SUD	Early Origin Memory (EOM)	SUD
Incident Caroline broke my confidence.	7	*Past Event*	

Step 4—Describe the emotional sensations you are feeling.

- When you think of the incident, what image disturbs you the most? For example, the way the person looked, or what they said, or what they did, or how they smelled.
- What *emotion or emotions* surface? *Focus on your feelings.*
- What *negative thought* goes along with it?
- Jot down in the second-row, under *Emotional,* words to describe how this incident makes you feel right now. (Try using The Feeling Wheel in Appendix B.)
- Give the incident a SUD number.
- Example: Caroline said the situation "makes me feel angry, betrayed, and embarrassed. I'm having a difficult time forgiving her." Her emotions felt like an 8.

Emotional Angry, betrayed, embarrassed unforgiving	8		

Step 5— Describe the physical sensations you are feeling.

- When you put together the image and the negative thought, what do you *feel in your body?*
- Where do you feel this disruption or disturbance in your body?
- Jot down in the third-row, under *Body,* words to describe how this incident physically makes you feel right now, then give it a SUD number.

If you feel your body change for the worse, we can conclude that the memory is raw and untreated.

Physical Fluttery tension in my chest; kind of sweaty.	8	

Step 6— Find a gaze point; Connect this event to a past event.

Find a point to gaze at to help you think. Recall I said there's a strong connection between the eyes and brain. Gazing is a reflection of the person looking deep inside themselves; to a far-off place in their unconscious. Notice where your eyes might be fixated in the room when you're thinking or talking about the most emotionally charged experiences; an experience with a relatively high SUD number. You may look at a couple of particular spots. Once you locate that spot, fix your gaze there.

- Find a gaze spot.
- Fixed on this spot, scan back into time.
- Go into your childhood first, and note the earliest memory that pops up *when you felt the exact same way.* Don't rule out a cultural memory.
- **Go wherever your mind takes you.** Don't direct your mind; let it just happen. Let Jesus take you where He wants you to go. Don't worry if it doesn't make sense to you. Your brain and Jesus know what to do. See what comes next, and after that.
- Go back to all the sights and sounds of the event.
- Now verbalize or write down what is going on internally and any memories that are emerging.
- Then rate how this memory feels on the SUD scale.
- Pick a few words to identify this childhood memory, including your age at the time. Write it in the column, "EOM."
  In this example, I recall telling my best friend Fiona that I peed in my pants on the bus. She promised not to tell anyone (breaking confidence). But she told Tommy who then started calling me "Pee-Pants." Then a bunch of other kids called me "Pee Pants." I felt mortified! And angry, betrayed, and ashamed.
- *Consider:* Is there *another* earlier life issue that might somehow be associated with this event? If so, note it in the EOM column.

This is your *Early Origin Memory (EOM).*

Event	SUD	EOM	SUD
Caroline broke my confidence.	4	Pee-Pants I age 7	7

Use the breathing and relaxation techniques, and prayer, to bring yourself back to your Jesus Safe and Calm place.

Now it's time to do your Work! Follow each step and record your responses on the worksheet on the next page, or you can use your own notebook.

Work-Steps: Locate an EOM in 6-Steps

Step 1—Prepare your mind, brain, and body.

Step 2—Bring up a recent disturbing event.

Step 3— Describe and record your responses regarding this event.

Step 4— Describe the emotional sensations you are feeling.

Step 5— Describe the physical sensations you are feeling.

Step 6— Find a gaze point; Connect this event to a possible past event.

Optional Prayer (Personalize as you feel lead)

Father, I understand now why I feel this way. Is there anything more You want to tell me? Help me to release the power this EOM has had over me, and my desire to (*name the behavior you want to avoid*). I surrender this memory and all disturbing emotions and body sensations to You. In Jesus's name.

Event	SUD	EOM	SUD
Incident (step 3)		*Past Event (step 6)*	
Emotions (step 4)		*Another connected past event?*	

Body (step 5)			

"Write to Heal" Notes or Prayer.

End of Session 1.

8

Detect Your Greatest Negative
Thoughts and Beliefs in 3-Steps
(Session 2)

Do you remember the first Rocky movie? Right before his match with heavyweight champion Apollo Creed, he tells his girlfriend Adrian that he doesn't have to win, he just needs to stay on his feet until the end. He says, "I just wanna prove somethin'—I ain't no bum."

I can relate. All my life I've been focused on trying to do well and look good because deep inside I'm trying to prove to myself, and everyone else, *I'm not a bum*. In other words, I'm trying to disprove my file cabinet of NTBs. How about you?

Keep in mind, *your brain treats every new experience as reality—until it's instructed to do otherwise.* When you experience a stressful feeling—anything from mild discomfort to intense sorrow, shame, rage or despair, *there is a specific thought causing your reaction,* whether you're conscious of it or not. This is why it is important to identify our primary NTBs.

In this session, you will be working these 3-steps:

1. Get to know the NTB categories.
2. Identify your primary NTBs.
3. Explain how these NTBSs affected you in the past and presently.

Optional Pre-Work Prayer (Personalize as you feel lead)
Father, You know me inside out. My thoughts are powerful. I believe there is no force or thought or belief in this world that is strong enough to hold me down when You enable me to change my mind to fit Your plan for my life. I ask for clarity and wisdom to clearly see the beliefs I've developed about myself in response to these adverse events. In Jesus's name.

Prepare your mind, brain, and body.

- Find your Jesus safe place; a place where you feel calm and grounded.
- Do some deep breathing until you feel ready and relaxed.
- Listen to your breathing. Don't try to slow or alter it.
- Breathe in God's goodness and love; breathe out any anxiety or fear.
- Do the eye movement exercises on page 73-74.

Work-Steps: Detect Your Greatest NTBs in 3-Steps

Step 1: Get to Know the NTB categories

There are three main thought and belief categories we'll work with which come out of a recognized psychotherapy called EMDR (which stands for *Eye Movement Desensitization and Reprocessing*).[42]

1. Defective personhood: *I am or I did something wrong or bad.*
2. Lack of safety and vulnerability: *I can't trust or feel safe.*
3. Lack of control and power: *I feel powerless and out of control.*

This "Greatest Hits List of Negative Thoughts and Beliefs" can help us pinpoint the memories that run us today. *Recognizing these statements as your own negative self-talk can help you link into memory networks containing untreated memories.*

Each NTB describes how we internalized a distressing event or moment. Usually the NTB began in childhood. Someone may have been uncaring, critical, absent, or abusive; or we may have misunderstood the situation. It's how we genuinely felt at that moment.

There is also a column of positive thoughts and beliefs (PTBs) which counter the negative ones. These are how you would feel *if* you'd gotten the opposite message. Rather than feeling defective or unsafe or powerless, for example, you would have felt worthy, safe, and confident. (You will use the PTB list in the next session.)

Some of these NTB's could fall into a different category, so don't get hung up on the category labels.

Do "The Work" and Get Past Your Past | 92

Note: Some women struggle with the opposite of negative thoughts and beliefs; they're minds are filled with *superior, "holy," righteous and prideful thinking*. If you recognize this is you (often multiple people will point this out) then identify the specific NTBs you need to work on.

Step 2: Identify Your Primary NTBs

In the last session, you identified *a present-day disturbing event* that currently bothers you. As you go through each category, *mark the primary NTBs you relate to the most that match the feelings that tie to this event.*

Let's say this is your situation, "Dad was drunk and driving erratically and I was in danger." Yes, this event disturbed you, yet it is not a negative thought or core belief. It's a description of something that happened.

To find your NTB, ask yourself:

- Dad was a drunk. *How did that make me feel?*
- What was the *prominent thought and belief* I attached to "dad was a drunk"?

Negative Thoughts and Belief Categories

1—Defective Personhood

This category is about feelings of shame; we have the feeling of being somewhat defective; a feeling of "I'm imperfect, a malfunctioned human being." While many of these feelings stem from childhood, some people's issues of shame took form in late adolescence or early adulthood due to adverse peer situations.

One night I met up with a guy friend at a bar. As usual I'd begun my journey to getting plastered. He took me to a small party at some dude's apartment where we continued to booze it up. I was led into a bedroom by one of the guys. Wasted and barely conscious, I didn't realize until hours later that four guys raped me.

The word spread like wild fire in the college dorm that I "pulled a train" (when a group of males, one after the other, have sex with a woman). My guy friend didn't stand up for me, and my peers ostracized and ignored me, presuming I "wanted it." To them, and to me, the only difference between me and a prostitute is I didn't exchange money. I felt covered inside and out with the vomit of humiliation and shame, and it wouldn't wash off no matter how many showers I took.

I don't know which felt worse—feeling defiled from the "gang rape" or the social judgment. Both were bad. Emotionally frozen, my only recourse was to keep this horrid incident a secret. Eventually I just became numb to being used and thrown out. I felt like a "bum." The way I felt was the way I acted. (I'm so glad this happened before phone cameras!)

My primary NTB's were: *I'm a bad person; I'm shameful; I'm permanently damaged.*

Negative Thought/Belief	Positive Thought/Belief
I don't deserve love; I'm not loved.	I deserve love; I am loved.
I'm a bad person.	I'm a good person.
I'm worthless and inadequate.	I'm worthy and worthwhile.
I'm shameful. (I'm a bum.)	I'm valuable and honorable.
I'm unlovable.	I'm lovable.
I'm not good enough; I don't deserve.	I'm deserving of good things.
I'm permanently damaged.	I'm healed.
I'm ugly; my body is unappealing.	I'm beautiful.
I'm stupid.	I'm smart and teachable.
I'm insignificant and unimportant.	I'm significant and important.
I'm a disappointment and a loser.	I'm victorious and strong.
I don't deserve to live.	I deserve to live fully.
I'm different and don't belong.	I'm perfect and acceptable.
I deserve to be miserable.	I deserve to be happy.

2—Lack of Safety and Vulnerability

Lack of safety and vulnerability are more than the obvious, "I feel unsafe. I fear being hurt." Feeling like a failure or incapable *is a response to fear and anxiety, which makes us feel unsafe* and colors our perception of the world and how capable we are in the world.

Even hearing about others being hurt, or watching a scary or evil movie, can impact and hurt us emotionally or physically. These fears can turn into feelings of lack of safety and become raw memories.

I remember anticipating the day that I'd get my driver's license, I'd sit in the garage and "fake drive" my dad's Dodge Dart. One day he noticed a dent on the side of the car. He automatically presumed I drove and dented it. I didn't know how to drive! He didn't believe me, yelled at me, then punished me for something I didn't do.

In other words, "I have no voice" and "My truth and emotions don't matter." My NTB said: *It's not safe to speak or feel; I can't trust adults.*

Negative Thought/Belief	Positive Thought/Belief
I cannot trust anyone.	I will choose whom to let in and trust. (Begin by trusting Jesus first.)
I'm in danger. I fear for my life.	I'm not in danger any longer.
I'm not safe.	I'm safe now.
It's not okay to speak or feel.	I can speak and show my emotions.
I'm afraid.	I'm no longer afraid.

3—Lack of Control and Power

This category has to do with the lack of ability to make positive choices, be heard, and the perceived inability to exert control in the world.

I had a bratty 9-year-old brother who found humor in sneaking up behind me and pulling down my pants. One day as I napped blissfully, he attacked. I kicked him off the bed. He flew face first onto the hardwood floor. His front tooth chipped in half. He darted out, opening a floodgate of tears. Then my father came in and declared, "You're grounded!" *Why?* "You're older and should know better." I felt angry, invalidated, and helpless. *I can't stand up for myself.*

Negative Thought/Belief	Positive Thought/Belief
I'm not in control —or— I'm a controller (as in control-freak!).	I have the right amount of control.
I'm powerless and helpless.	I have choices I can make.
I can't get what I want and need.	I can get what I want and need.
I can't stand up for myself.	I can stand up and speak for myself.
I can't trust myself.	I can learn to trust myself.
I will fail; I cannot succeed.	I will succeed.

I have to be perfect.	I can be myself and make mistakes.
I can't handle it.	I can handle it.
I can't trust anyone.	I will choose whom to let in and trust.

Regarding the first NTB and PTB thought: "I'm not in control" or "I'm a controller" → "I have the right amount of control." We are never really in control, are we? Jeremiah 10:23 states, *"I know, LORD, that our lives are not our own. We are not able to plan our own course."* Proverbs 19:21 and 16:9 also states, *"You can make many plans, but the LORD's purpose will prevail; We can make our own plans, but the LORD gives the right answer."*

Despite the fact we are never really in control, we have the knowledge and hope that God's power and control far surpasses what we can do on our own. Knowing God is in control of our lives is a reason to feel safe, secure, and empowered—it's the "right amount of control."

Step 3: Explain how these NTBs affected you in the past and presently.

How has the NTB affected your life in general—in the past and presently?

- Is there a particular *image* that comes to your mind?
- How do you *treat and talk to yourself* when you believe this thought?
- How do you *treat and talk to others* when you believe this thought?

Dad instilled in my mind that "I have no control over my life." Trying to defend myself didn't work. I felt powerless and helpless. This is exactly how I felt each time as an adult I experienced a significant life change because my adolescent feeling of lack of power and control linked up to a present-day experience.

It's time to do your Work!

Work-Steps: Detect Your Greatest NTBs in 3-Steps

Step 1: Get to Know the NTB categories

Jot down anything that comes to your mind as you read through the categories.

Step 2: Identify Your Primary NTBs. (Don't tackle more than three.)

1.

2.

3.

> **Step 3:** Explain how these NTBs affected you in the past and presently.

End of Session 2.

9

Change a Negative Thought and Belief in 6-Steps
(Session 3)

Facebook announced it is funding research on a project to read the human mind—a machine that can pick up your thoughts directly from your neurons and translate them into words. The aim, said the company, is to allow us to control our digital devices by the power of thought.[43]

Everything about that is troubling, yet consider: If someone could pick up and translate your thoughts into words, how many of those words would be Scripture ... or a deadly NTB?

Trauma, ACEs, and dysfunctional relationships train us accustomed to focus on our failures, our supposed stupidity, and worthlessness. We lose sight of our true value and abilities. Winston Churchill once said, "Every fool can see what is wrong. See what is good in it." In other words, I look at myself and see what's wrong, which means I'm a fool. The truth is: God looks at me and see's what's right! *For real transformation to occur, we need to experience who we are as defined by God.*

Thinking patterns and beliefs, and consequently lifestyle patterns, will not change without new input. How do we build a new core belief? By identifying the inaccurate false belief and calling out the lie, and then replacing it with truth. There's a saying in neuroscience: *Neurons that fire together wire together.* This means the more you run a neurocircuit in your brain, the stronger that circuit becomes. The more you practice something, the stronger those circuits get.[44]

We must create new neural pathways of thinking. God wants to load a brand-new software program into your mind, one that He's designed specifically for you. In this session, you will be coached to lay down a new set of thoughts and beliefs—PTBs—that lead you naturally to think on that which is good and truthful. "Your mission, should you choose to accept it," is to become aware of, and then quickly capture the deceptive thought; investigate it, and reframe it with truth by repetitively adding positive input into your mind.

You will be coached through 6-steps and to write out exactly what comes to your mind.

1. Name your NTB.
2. Establish the EOM and NTB connection.
3. Focus on the NTB. What emotions arise?
4. Describe how your body feels; it's reaction.
5. Question and investigate the truth of the NTB.
6. Create a new PTB; a new truthful thinking track.

We can't lump the primary NTBs all together and process them as one. Tackle one NTB at a time. Again, before doing The Work, read through each step and the questions.

Prepare your mind, brain, and body.

- Find your Jesus safe place; a place where you feel calm and grounded.
- Do some deep breathing until you feel ready and relaxed.
- Listen to your breathing. Don't try to slow or alter it.
- Breathe in God's goodness and love; breathe out any anxiety or fear.
- Do the eye movement exercises on page 73-74.

Work-Steps: Change an NTB in 6-Steps

Step 1—Name your NTB.

Name your NTB—*the primary one you believe impacts your life the most today.*

Step 2—Establish the EOM and NTB connection.

- Go back to your EOM from session #1.
- What connection do you see between the memory of the event and this NTB? What does your mind see?
- Did you think of another earlier time where you felt this way?
- Go to your Jesus safe and calm place.

Step 3—Focus on the NTB. What emotions arise?

Use "The Feeling Wheel" in Appendix B to help you express your emotions if you need to.

- Note the *emotions* that surface when you believe this NTB.
- When you "listen" carefully to the emotion, what do you hear?
- How do you *act out* this emotion?
- What coping or defense mechanisms do you tend to use?

Step 4—Describe how your body feels; it's reaction.

- When you bring to the surface the NTB and EOM, does your body feel uncomfortable? Explain. For example, does the NTB cause your breathing to change (shorten, quicken, etc.)?
- What physical sensations surface (i.e., blood pressure rises, get nauseous, hands start to shake, headachy, experience insomnia.)?
- If, for example, you feel "a knot in your stomach," concentrate on that knot and on the sensations. Visualize untying the knot.
- Take some deep breaths; pray and ask Jesus to help you let go of the sensations.

Step 5—Question and investigate the truth of the NTB.

The Bible talks about the importance of mental habits and discipline,

> *We **demolish arguments** and every pretension that sets itself up against the knowledge of God, and **we take captive every thought** to make it obedient to Christ (2 Corinthians 10:5).*

Instead of automatically finding evidence to support our NTB, we're going to work with the Holy Spirit and put our core belief against the truth; we "take it captive." We take the time to inquire, look for proof, and dig deeper. This is called "disputing." We're in essence asking God, *In what ways am I looking at this all wrong? What are the facts?*

Answer these questions:

- Can I be absolutely certain my NTB is true?
- What kind of proof do I have this is *absolutely* true?
- Does God's Word and truth support this belief?
- Evidence supporting it is:
- Evidence contradicting it is:
- Can I conclude that my thought is accurate?

If your belief is based on another person's remark, such as, "you'll always be lazy," ask yourself and Jesus: *Based on this person's character and flaws, can he/she really be believed? What proof does he/she have that I'll always be lazy?*

What if the NTB is true?

Example belief: "My father has never loved me." In your investigation, you find out that your father intentionally distanced himself from you because you reminded him of his "awful and noxious" ex-wife, your mother. Unfortunately, this is true. Instead of substantiating all the reasons why your father is right to not love you, seek reality. *Do not take his stuff on yourself.*

- Give yourself credit for having the courage to seek the truth. No matter the outcome, you were brave, open, and on the right path.
- You now have an explanation as to why you think a certain way and do the things you do. You can move forward. *It's his loss.*
- Reflect on Dr. Lisa Najavits's comment, *"The most painful truth is better in the long run than the most positive lie."*[45]
- Ask yourself: "What's the worst that can happen?"

Step 6—Create a PTB; a new truthful thinking track.

Think of this step as *reframing* an NTB. We want to reframe an NTB and/or event to one that can generate more positive thoughts and feelings. Any lies and inaccurate thoughts must be reinterpreted and replaced with truth. The Bible gives us precise instructions in Philippians 4:8 regarding restructuring our thoughts.

> *Whatever is true, whatever is noble, honorable, whatever is right, whatever is pure, whatever is lovely, whatever is admirable—if anything is excellent or praiseworthy— think about such things* (Philippians 4:8).

The Message puts it this way:
I'd say you'll do best by filling your minds and meditating on things true, noble, reputable, authentic, compelling, gracious—the best, not the worst; the beautiful, not the ugly; things to praise, not things to curse.

These qualities are what I call "soul food" for the mind. *Whatever we focus upon increases,* which is why the phrase "think about such things" is critical. We're being asked to take some kind of action—to concentrate our attention on; let our mind dwell on that which is good. Notice the first quality mentioned to think on is truth. All these qualities to think on are only found in God's Word.

In the next verse Paul says, *"Whatever you have learned or received or heard from me, or seen in me—**put it into practice**. And the God of **peace will be with you**"* (4:9). Meditating and applying Scripture can close down some NTB files and create new positive files. The result: we focus on positive outcomes in life, and our stress response system decreases—because when the Word of God is coursing through our mind 24/7, it keeps our thoughts filtered and pure and clean.

As John Stott said, "We must allow the Word of God to confront us, to disturb our security, to undermine our complacency and to overthrow our patterns of thought and behavior." As you read, pause frequently to meditate on the meaning of what you are reading. Absorb the Word into your system by dwelling on it, pondering it, going over it again and again in your mind, considering it from many different angles, until it becomes part of you.

I call this *deliberate rumination*—we continually focus on positive outcomes and changing our perspectives about ourselves, others, and the world; we avoid seeing crises as insurmountable.

As James Hood Wilson put it, *"Strive to be like Christ. Ask the question: Would Christ have done as I am doing—spoken as I am speaking, felt as I am feeling? Am I like Christ in this?"*

Turn a Lie (NTB) into a PTB

Decades ago, when my dad called me a "fat piggy" I internalized and believed it. My NTBs were:

- I'm ashamed.
- I'm unlovable.
- I'm ugly; my body is awful.

Healing meant changing my shame-talk and investigating this statement. *Was it true?* I believed it was. I could see the fat in the mirror.

Could I be absolutely certain it was true? Upon further investigation, I recognized I was a little overweight, but I'd never been the image of obesity I'd created in my mind. I was just fine. Dad's critical labels made him the liar. My PTB: *My dad's critical tongue has nothing to do with me. He needs to see a therapist and work out his issues. I have a heavenly Father who loves me so much and sees me as perfect.*

Let's say you believe, "I'm such a loser!" *If your best friend or child made the same statement, how would you answer?* Would you say you speak to yourself in the same way you do someone you respect and/or love? Would you agree and tell her, "You're right! You're a huge failure"? No. You'd probably answer compassionately. Be your own best friend or child!

Create a PTB Exercise (G.R.O.W: God Restores Our Worth)

A Randy Glasbergen comic goes, "Your resume here says that you are created in the image of God. Very impressive!" It's a fact: *Knowing and believing God's Word will change a person's life.* No lie; no deception; no defense mechanism can remain intact in the presence of God's Word.

Someone else's misusing or rejecting us does not negate or change who we are—valuable human beings—worthy of love, respect, and purpose. Then there are some of us who don't really believe God likes us. I've heard some women say, "I know God loves me because He created me, but I don't think He really likes me." Nothing could be further from the truth. Remember, whatever we have done—past, present, and future—has been forgiven and forgotten by God.

God "likes" you just the way you are, yet He wants the very best for you which is why He continually takes His children through the transformation process. There's nothing we can do to ever lose His love. The Scriptures prove it. With a more biblical understanding of ourselves, the stress response system calms down, which translates into lesser or resolved physical and emotional issues. We can experience a new self, and be content with only seeking God's acceptance.

However, if we don't have faith in the author of the Word, and in who we really are, then we won't experience much change; we won't be able to adequately deprogram our brains of NTBs and misbeliefs. Consequently, our true identity will never permeate our mind and become part of our lives. Consider this: If you don't believe what God says about you in the Bible, essentially, you're calling Him a liar!

We usually aren't who we think we are because of what has been seared into our minds and brains. We must *experience* what God says about us concretely and vividly. A.W. Tozer wrote, "True faith requires that we believe everything that God has said about himself, but also that we believe everything he has said about us!"[46]

To change your mind's trajectory, the next time a toxic memory pops up, pair that negative message or belief with the truth of Scripture, thereby, changing the thought and creating a new memory.

What I want you to do next is:
*   Find the PTB on pages 94-96 that counteracts your NTB.

- Attach a Scripture that supports the PTB. You can use this biblical PTB list.
- Ask Jesus: "What would a person with this PTB naturally think and do?"
- Then create in your mind this new experience and memory by *visualizing it as reality*.
- Close your eyes and observe how you feel about the truth.

Biblical PTBs

This is who you truly are:

- I am beautiful (Song of Songs 4:7).
- I am radiant (Psalm 34:4).
- I am "complete" because God lives in me (Colossians 2:9-10).
- I have the highest possible value (Psalm 8:5; Genesis 1:27).
- I am fearfully ("awesome") and brilliantly made (Psalm 139:14).
- I am born of God. The evil one cannot touch me (1 John 5:18).
- I am the apple of God's eye (Deuteronomy 32:10).
- I am a beloved child (Ephesians 5:1)
- I am brand new (2 Corinthians 5:17).
- I have a mind like Jesus Christ (1 Corinthians 2:16).
- I am God's child (John 1:12).
- I am Christ's friend (John 15:15).
- I am forgiven; my sins have been taken away (Romans 3:23-24).
- I am free from condemnation (Romans 8:1-2).
- I am a conqueror; *a survivor* (Romans 8:37).
- I cannot be separated from the love of God (Romans 8:38-39).
- I am a saint (1 Corinthians 1:2)
- My heart has been cleansed from a guilty conscious (Heb. 10:22).
- I am holy, blameless, covered with God's love (Ephesians 1:4).
- I am transformed (*sanctified*) by God's presence (Ephesians 1:1).
- I have the favor of God (Proverbs 8:35)
- I am one spirit with Jesus (Galatians 3:28; 1 Corinthians 6:17).
- I am the salt and light of the earth (Matthew 5:13-14).
- I am blessed with every spiritual blessing (Ephesians 1:3).
- I have been adopted as God's child (Ephesians 1:5-6).
- I am God's work of art; His masterpiece (Ephesians 2:10).
- I have direct access to God (Ephesians 2:18; 3:12).
- I am confident because of God's work in me (Philippians 1:6).
- I can do anything through Christ's strength (Philippians 4:13).

God wants us to not only know the wonder of being made in His image, but to experience it at a soul level. Don't worry if you can't fully grasp these truths at first about yourself, none of us can.

Optional Prayer (Personalize as you feel lead)
Lord God, help me to reset the image I have of myself and embrace myself as the unique, powerful, and beautiful woman you created me to be. I believe I am Your perfect workmanship (Ephesians 2:10). In Jesus's name.

It's time to do your Work!

Work-Steps: Change an NTB in 6-Steps

Step 1—Name your NTB.

Step 2— Establish the EOM and NTB connection.

Step 3— Focus on the NTB. What emotions arise?

Step 4—Describe how your body feels; it's reaction.

Step 5—Question and investigate the truth of the NTB.

- <u>Can I be absolutely certain my NTB is true?</u>

- <u>What kind of proof do I have this is *absolutely* true?</u>

- <u>Does God's Word and truth support this belief? (If yes, document it.)</u>

- <u>Evidence supporting my NTB is:</u>

- <u>Evidence contradicting NTB is:</u>

- <u>Can I conclude that my thought is accurate?</u>

Step 6—Create a new PTB; a new truthful thinking tract.

The PTB that counteracts my NTB is:

Scripture that supports my PTB is:

Additional "Create a New PTB" Exercises
The Power of "I Am" Exercise

"It breaks my heart when women look at the sky and think, "Wow! God is amazing!" but look in the mirror and say, "ugh!" As if he did not make both."

–Stasi Eldrege

Have you ever *really* thought about the power of the words "I am"? Do you truly recognize the subconscious "I am" statements that you are holding about yourself? "I am" is one of the most powerful statements we can make. It's more powerful than "I have" or "I can." Whatever follows "I am" starts the creation of it.

God told Moses His name is "I Am" (Exodus 3:14). Numerous times both God and Jesus used "I am" statements about themselves. They were making a powerful claim pointing to their divinity. Obviously, we're not professing to be God, but when we make a claim "I am …" we are claiming *to be* a person of worthiness.

When king David proclaimed, *"**I am** fearfully and wonderfully made"* (Psalm 139:14), he was acknowledging that he was fashioned by *the* Master's hand; that he was created remarkable, unique, and valuable.

To dissolve the cognitive dissonance in our core belief system, we need to hit the "reset" button. Write down or state out loud:

- I AM made in the magnificent and vibrant image of God
- I AM my own unique person; waiting to unfold and be expressed.
- I AM a radiant center of God-thoughts and feelings.
- I AM courageous enough to be myself.
- I AM [*state what comes to your mind*] …

I suggest that for the next month, take one statement a day from the list of biblical PTBs and meditate on it; grapple with it; study it; visualize it as reality. *Then write out all the evidence to support this belief.*

For example, the first one is: "I am beautiful."

- This is true because God says so.
- My neighbor told me I was so kind to bring her flowers from my garden. She said, "You're beautiful."

- My heart is no longer hardened towards certain people. This makes me beautiful (inside beauty).

Then complete this sentence: "Because [*the statement*] this means I can … For example: Because *I am beautiful,* I can walk into the room with confidence. What do you notice about each of these statements? They are positive and not condemning. They tell you "you can" and not "you can't." They are Jesus's words—truth.

Don't worry if you can't fully grasp these truths about yourself; no one can at first. We may intellectually get it, and believe God said it, but it takes time and God's supernatural intervention to experience these truths about ourselves. *We need to unite these truths with faith.*

Through practice and Scripture meditation, God's Word will re-route our thinking patterns. We can pair our negative thinking belief with the truth of Scripture, thereby, *creating a new memory.*

Develop a Thankful and Grateful Spirit

One way to change an NTB is to practice gratitude—and make it a conscious everyday effort. People who are grateful are healthier, happier, and more optimistic. They have a better functioning brain and heart, and peace. It's no surprise the Bible has long embraced gratitude as an indispensable spiritual virtue.

Countless scientific studies bear that thankfulness and gratitude as an essential component of health, wholeness, and well-being. It protects us from developing a "woe is me" attitude. It's harder for seeds of crankiness or criticism or depression or anger to take root in a grateful heart.

Scripture says, "*I will give repeated thanks to the LORD, praising him to everyone (Psalm 109:30).* Notice the word "repeated." But what about when things don't turn out, like disasters, accidents, abuse, job losses or cancer? The Bible instructs us to *"give thanks in all circumstances, for this is God's will for you in Christ Jesus" (1 Thessalonians 5:18).* Notice the verse does not say to give thanks *for* all circumstances, but to give thanks *in* all circumstances. There's a big difference.

Being thankful in a dreadful circumstance can only be done by faith because it goes against our flesh nature. We can choose to pray, "Father,

I'm in a bad place right now. I don't want to be here, but You, in your love and wisdom allowed it for me. I thank You for what You're about to do. Thank you that You've got the perfect plan for me (Jeremiah 29:11). Thank you also for …" We can always find something to be thankful for in the face of adversity.

End of Session 3.

10

Update and Renew an Early Origin Memory in 6-Steps
(Session 4)

Receiving continual software updates for our computers and phones is a customary part of life now. These updates contain important changes to improve the performance, stability, and security of the applications that run on our computers and phones, ensuring they will continue to run safely and efficiently. Updating is good! This is what we want to do with those EOMs—early origin memories—*update and renew*. A processed adverse memory turns into a "memory."

"Positive affirmations" and "positive psychology" are popular for a good reason. Neuropsychologists state that when two things are held in the mind at the same time, they start to connect with each other. This is why talking about hard things with someone who's encouraging and supportive can be so healing: *The painful feelings and memories get infused with the comfort, encouragement and closeness you experience with the other person.* God gives us friends, family, and a support system for a reason—to refresh and revive our memories and spirits.

Positive experiences and declarations can be used to soothe, balance, reframe, and even replace negative ones. We know that adding new truthful, positive messages and images to a sad, angry, or shameful memory, for example, can propel a person out of a negative state because the memory has been changed; it's been updated and renewed.

In this last session we will be focusing on restructuring anxious memories that repeatedly surface in our conscious; those bothersome memories that keep popping up when we least desire.

Updating an EOM

Recall I said that if other things are in your mind at the same time that you call up a particular memory—and if they're strongly pleasant or unpleasant—the brain automatically puts them together—like two puzzle pieces. When the memory leaves the conscious, it is stored along with those other associations. The next time the (revised) memory is activated, *it will tend to bring those associations with it.*

When a powerful EOM emerges, we want to look at it from an empowered position. So, we update it by adding something positive. This requires a conscious effort. Example:

- A disturbing memory surfaces. →
- *Mind develops an action plan:* Chooses *not* to ruminate on the negative experience and/or "medicate" in some way. →
- *Thinks:* "I need to be with someone who can console and listen to me," or "I need more information." →
- *Action:* Calls a friend or pastor; and/or gathers truthful and helpful information; and/or recalls a positive experience. →
- Creates new positive image. →
- Attaches and links into the old image/memory. →
- *Result:* The adverse memory is updated and restructured (processed); toxic body and mind effects are minimized.

Important: Unless we choose to alter the upsetting memory by adding something good to it, we will always go to our unconscious default reactions, which typically results in increased toxic thinking and destructive acting out.

Let me be clear: Reframing and updating our memories in no way takes away from the truth that a harmful event occurred, and that grief and outrage may be significant components. It certainly doesn't dismiss that a person who causes harm must be accountable for the offense.

Example: Felicia's Work

Felicia needed to confront and treat her distressful memory of losing her virginity to a rapist (her step-dad). She needed to unearth and infuse into her existing memory the truth and positive information.

- I'm so angry and sad I lost my virginity. I find myself angry a lot and ruminating on the rape, and the unfairness at the loss of my innocence. → *Reframes with truth and reality* →

- I'm mourning the loss of not being able to experience a real "first time," and a feeling of closeness to my mate, as well as the experience of the awkwardness, the surprise, and excitement. Grieving is good. → *Adds a truthful and positive image to the memory* →

- I've learned that given my age and the circumstances, I was incapable of consenting. My step-dad committed a crime, yet he's made me feel imprisoned. I didn't give him permission to have with sex me. My virginity was taken from me and that wasn't my fault. I was the victim. It's okay to feel sad and broken. → *Adds another true positive image* →

- I also learned some people don't see a torn hymen as lost virginity. They believe it isn't a physical state but a spiritual, emotional, relational state; a state when the person gives consent and chooses to be with another person. Rape is not sex. It's an act of violence. They're not the same. I can, in the future, experience the excitement and awkwardness of a "first time!" → *Adds another true positive image* →

- Since that awful day there have been many things I've done right, like breaking the secret! *The truth shall set you free!* (John 8:32) →

- *Result:* Distressing memory has been literally updated and changed; NTBs have converted to PTBs.

Restructuring Practices

There are several sources we can go to uncover, and consequently add, truthful and positive information to change a distressful memory:

1. Ask for God's counsel in prayer and Bible study.
2. Seek safe and godly counsel.
3. Power of visualization.
4. Put responsibility on the right person.
5. Judge favorably.

Ask for God's Counsel in Prayer and Bible Study

"Then you will call on me and come and pray to me, and I will listen to you" (Jeremiah 29:12).

When we are struggling, we go to God with our question and concerns; seeking direction (called prayer). When we get alone with God—waiting silently and expectantly, where the intrusions of life can't interfere, where human opinions can't touch us, we receive a deeper insight into His nature and heart of love, which will get us through the darkness—and change a disturbing thought and memory into a peaceful one. This is why there are "optional Prayers" sprinkled throughout The Work. Adding Bible study, only strengthens The Work and the brain. The Word of God is medicinal and nourishment for the mind. It's been said that if you have a Bible that's falling apart, then you'll have a life that's not falling apart.

Seek Safe and Godly Counsel

One of the bravest things a soul can do is share her story of pain. It's a critical step in healing. There is more power in sharing our weaknesses than our strengths. I love what Karen Salmonsohn said, "Sometimes you just need to talk about something—not to get sympathy or help, but just to kill its power by allowing the truth of things to hit the air."

Experts found that people who have been exposed to crises and have supportive relationships that provide care, encouragement love and trust are protected against developing PTSD. Talking through experiences and providing first aid to others allows us to convert traumatic experiences into *post-adverse growth* and *resilience*.[47]

Ecclesiastes 4:12 states, *"A person standing alone can be attacked and defeated, but two can stand back-to-back and conquer. Three are even better, for a triple-braided cord is not easily broken."* And Colossians 3:16 says, *"Teach and counsel each other with all the wisdom he gives."*

The Power of Visualization

Research has shown that mentally visualizing or rehearsing a particular situation can be extremely useful for overcoming a negative core belief. By adding the power of our imagination to a distressing memory, we can visualize a future positive event by creatively changing an old mind and memory script.

Dr. Caroline Leaf explains, "The way you use your conscious and nonconscious mind (your imagination) shifts the way the brain processes information. So, as you visualize something, your thinking changes, which, in turn, changes your brain waves and engages different neural pathways, called *directed neuroplasticity*."[48]

Imagine a Shield Around Your Mind

If you find yourself ruminating over something stressful, visualize a shield around your mind and thoughts. You say, "I'm not going to absorb these toxic emotions that are threatening me. Jesus's shield of protection is all around me. I'm safe; I'm calm; I have peace."

Jamie and Kara

Jamie has many disturbing memories of her ex-husband controlling her, so she used visualization to prepare for an upcoming meeting with him.

> In the past, when I had to meet with my ex, I'd become a wreck. All the old memories of his abuse and control came flooding out. So, I imagined myself strong; a powerful successful business woman. I saw myself walking into that meeting with my head high, shoulders back, and projecting tremendous confidence! Everything about me communicated I was tough, secure, in control, and emotionally stable. I could feel my arms and legs and shoulder muscles; they were solid. I saw myself interacting with him competently and in complete control.

This new image of empowerment updated Jamie's memory of feeling anxious and helpless in the presence of her ex. It gave her the courage to confidently and boldly meet with him when it was necessary.

Kara has problems giving presentations to her clients due to past memories of failing and not feeling she has ever been good enough to be taken seriously. Prior to each presentation, she imagines that Jesus is kicking off the presentation. They are a team. She visualizes every person's eyes riveted on Jesus's every word. Then He asks Kara to step in and take over.

In her mind, she takes the same powerful stance as Jesus. Every person's eyes move onto her. Her peripheral vision is keenly aware of Jesus beaming, "That's my girl!" She ran a movie in her mind of handling this challenging situation victoriously from start to finish.

Kara also recognized that a big fear of giving presentations came from an EOM that her grandfather instilled in her father—*Work hard and do it perfect!* She learned that all God asks her to do is her very best and He will do the rest. (This is what I call a *spirit of excellence* versus a *spirit of perfection.*)

By using visualization regularly, Kara began to put things in perspective. She made her work a ministry versus a job. Jesus helped her to simply enjoy what she was doing.

"So, we can say with confidence, "The LORD is my helper, so I will have no fear. What can mere people do to me?" (Hebrews 13:6).

Basic Visualization Steps

- Relax your body and take several long slow breaths.
- Now focus on a future situation you'd like to see happen.
- Run a movie in your mind of handling this challenging situation victoriously from start to finish. Place Jesus in your movie strategically.
- Focus on what you're seeing, thinking, and feeling.
    o What do you see?
    o What do you feel?
    o How are you behaving; projecting yourself?
    o What do you believe about yourself; about the situation?
- Focus on the powerful positive image.
- Feel the positive emotions and body sensations.
- If applicable, move yourself into the posture that goes with the image (i.e. standing tall and firm).

Visualize Changing Physical Symptoms

This may help if you have physical symptoms that are bothering you:

- Focus on the part of your body that is the issue.

- How does it feel to you?
- Imagine what it looks like internally.
- Is there a sound or temperature associated with it? If so, what?
- Now imagine Jesus's power—His Light and Life—beaming through the top of your head and touching this part of your body.
- Hold this image as long as possible.
- Feel the Light touching that body part, changing and healing it.
- Describe how it feels.

Creatively Change a Nightmare

After a nightmare, we try to forget it as quickly as possible in order to escape any fear or anxiety. Re-imagining the dream can actually change some aspect of it so it's no longer intrusive and scary. Try it.

Pick a recent nightmare. Creatively change (visualize) the dream any way you like so that it feels good and right. Then rehearse the new version of the dream in your mind for a few minutes, a few times a day. Continue this for about a week. Some people find it helpful to write it out or record it on their phone.

Put Responsibility on the Right Person

For anyone who's been abused or violated, or persistently criticized, there are often feelings of shame, unworthiness, and guilt, along with feelings of lack of safety and power. Many believe they brought on the situation themselves, which is a lie.

To kill the lie, we need to figure out who is responsible for our pain and put the burden of the offense on the right person. Then we can change the memory of the offense. Don't discount it may go back a generation or more. If you're not sure, ask God, "Who laid these lies into my soul. Who caused this pain?" In other words, "Who's responsible?"

Consider what Jesus, the greatest therapist who ever lived, said:

The things that come out of the mouth come from the heart, and these make a man 'unclean.' For out of the heart come evil thoughts, murder, adultery, sexual immorality, theft, false testimony, slander. These are what make a man 'unclean' (Matthew 15:18-20).

The very descriptive Message version translates it,

What comes out of the mouth gets its start in the heart. It's from the heart that we vomit up evil arguments, murders, adulteries, fornications, thefts, lies, and cussing. That's what pollutes.

Some people torment us into believing we're dirty, unworthy, and unacceptable to God and to others, and we're to blame. In biblical times, this condition was called "unclean." Unclean translated means "impure," or "pollutes," as *The Message* Bible translates it. Impurities—emotional or chemical—pollute the body and desecrate God's temple, which is us.

In the Old Testament, one of the things God considered "unclean" was death, and throughout the book of Leviticus we read that contact with death brings uncleanliness. How appropriate since misused power and control brings about death.

"Unclean" is also equated to "filthy rags" (Isaiah 64:6). When we love another person, and that person has power and authority over us, we tend to take the person's "unclean" dirty words and internalize them; believe they are truth, yet they are filthy rags.

Jesus is saying: *It's not what goes in my mouth that defiles me; it's what comes out of my mouth and heart that defiles me.* The mouth reveals most clearly the condition of the heart, and thereby behavior. Therefore, if another person spews their verbal vomit onto me—calls me a *blah ... blah ... blah,* they cannot destroy my soul with their tongue, or make me feel contaminated because the verbal vomit came out of *their* mouth; it came out of *their* heart.

Jesus said, *"Don't be afraid of those who want to kill your body; they cannot touch your soul"* (Matthew 10:28). The only thing that can dirty me is what comes from inside of my heart. According to Jesus:

Offender = Unclean. Victim = Clean.

Offender = Guilty. Victim = Innocent.

No one and nothing can make you an outcast, dirty, or untouchable. People can't; the sins of your family can't; abusers can't. Remember: The heart is connected to the mouth. Only if the heart is changed, can the words which come out of the mouth change.

Tell your soul: *I am the one who decides if another person's statement about me has power over me or not. Me only — and God's Word.* Other people's evil words only taint themselves and make them filthy.

Jesus also said, *"A good tree* (the victim) *cannot bear bad fruit, and a bad tree* (the offender) *cannot bear good fruit"* (Matthew 7:18).

Let this sink in and the image you have of yourself: Even if you've had contact with an unclean person (creating an "unclean" memory), as a Christian, *you cannot bear bad or evil things. You are not your NTB! The NTB belongs to the offender.*

Update your memory with this good news! Grasping the truth of Jesus's words doesn't change what happened, but it does change our perceptions of the event; it doesn't rewrite the past, but it does rewrite the brain by rewriting a shame-based sense of self.

Second Corinthians 5:17 confirms that *you are a new creation in Christ.* You have been made new spiritually by the power of God. *The old life is gone; a new life has begun!"* You get a life do-over.

The phrase "in Christ" is used quite often in the Bible (John 14:20; 17:23). It means we have Him and His power constantly working within our mind and body to transform us. He gives us exactly what we need, at the right time, to be victorious.

Judge Favorably

Today many of us are struggling with different forms of anger and unforgiveness, a direct result of an earlier memory. If you have read any of my recent books, you know I'm an advocate of "judging favorably." I believe that if we ask God to help us see a situation differently, He will enable us to change our perceptions and our memories constructively.

Jewish culture has emphasized the need to "judge favorably" for thousands of years. The rabbis declared that "judging others in favorable terms" is as important as visiting the sick, praying, or teaching the Scriptures to your children.

Jenna conveyed to her therapist, "I now realize the person who hurt me is a victim and suffering with his own pain. He didn't realize he caused me suffering because he was too blinded and wounded himself. His attempts to control me were his mind's way of trying to feel important and secure." Jenna reframed the event in a positive direction. She judged favorably.

Scripture reminds us, *"Make allowance for each other's faults"* (Colossians 3:13); *"For all have sinned and fall short of the glory of God. ... There is no one righteous, not even one"* (Romans 3:10; 23). We can choose to let go of and forgive a flawed human being who did a very bad thing (or things) as a consequence of their own wounding and flawed belief system.

May this truth give you some peace, *"... on the day of judgment people will give an account for every careless word they speak ...* (Matthew 12:36). All offenders will be accountable for their actions!

Let the Steam Out of the Memory

What we need to recognize is our perspective on a particular situation may seem right and logical, but is always limited. For example, Tanya's struggles and fears as an adult go back to when her dad left her and her mom at age six. She vividly remembers him driving off, believing he didn't care. She prayed, *God, bring all the relevant information about this experience to my mind.* She then had an extremely vivid image of the anguish that was on her dad's face as he drove away.

A flood of understanding and relief filled her when she finally realized that leaving his daughter that day pained him greatly. This encouraged her to have a conversation with him about that day (she had refused to have anything to do with him since then). When they talked, she learned about the ongoing conflicts between him and her mom, and how he felt leaving was something he had to do to benefit them both. She got a view of the full picture and discarded her cropped view.

As one writer brilliantly stated, "Judgement will always reduce the size of the frame." When we're in pain it's easy to lose perspective. The circumstances and intensity of our suffering can keep us from seeing the bigger picture.

I challenge you not to put your own frame of perception and judgment around your memories. Harper Lee wrote, "You never really understand a person until you consider things from his point of view . . . Until you climb inside of his skin and walk around in it."

No healthy and functional person wakes up one day and decides to hurt or abuse or offend another person. It's never a black and white issue; we have a limited perspective. *Broken hurt people— hurt people; broken hurt people—raise broken people.*

Forgiveness

Three-year-old Hollee was arguing with her mom during bedtime. In frustration, her mother spit out, "I'm done with you. Go to sleep!" to which Hollee responded, "Mommy, I forgive you." Mom didn't know Hollee even knew the word *forgive,* so she asked what she meant. Hollee said, "It means you were wrong, and I'm tired of being mad, and now I'm going to sleep and my heart won't have a tummy ache."

That says it all, doesn't it? When we forgive someone, we aren't condoning their actions. We're saying we're tired of being mad, and we're ready to let go of the fury so our heart won't ache and can finally heal. Forgiveness means "to excuse, to pardon to remit or cancel." *It's giving up our right to get the person back.* Yes, it's hard, but is possible through the power of Christ. If He tells us to do something, He will enable us to do so.

When Jesus called out asking forgiveness for those who nailed Him to the cross, He modeled to every one of us compassion, mercy, and absolution. We choose to work to show His heart of kindness by forgiving those who may have wronged us. The result: We heal.

It's amazing how our NTBs will change when we begin to bless and pray for those who've hurt us. We can lift them up to God and visualize what an awesome person they could be if they had a genuine relationship with Jesus. He can so transform our hearts that instead of wishing evil upon them, we desire good for them. We can change an NTB to a PTB.

What we're talking about is a biblical concept called *unconditional acceptance.* Jesus said, "*Do not judge others* [unfavorably], *and you will not be judged. Do not condemn others, or it will all come back against you. Forgive others, and you will be forgiven"* (Luke 6:37).

Unconditional acceptance understands condemning and judging unfavorably is not our job. When we choose to forgive and judge favorably, we reprocess a bad memory into a better memory. It's a much better solution. It all begins with the *decision* to work towards forgiveness.

Forgiveness is not a "one and done" deal. *The deeper the wound, the longer the process. Yet ... we are able because God is able.* Don't worry if your emotions don't follow right away; God will honor your decision to let go of the offense.

Judge Yourself Favorably

Self-blame is a common response to being abandoned or rejected or abused. We tend to assume responsibility for something that *happened to us*; yet, we did nothing wrong. No doubt, pain is the cause of our actions. Therefore, we need to reframe, reinterpret and apply the same principles about judging another person favorably to ourselves.

One last clarification: there is no guarantee that you'll never return to older feelings. It is not uncommon to be triggered by something, and then strongly feel the rage again. This is part of the natural fight/flight response; a healthy response to violation that is wired in us. *This does not mean that you have not forgiven the person.* For these complicated reasons, it's vital to take your feelings immediately to Jesus, read Scripture, and talk to a safe person. The objective is to create a positive experience that can connect to the triggered memory, thereby updating it.

Optional Prayer (Personalize as you feel lead)

Father, I let go of the person who hurt me and the lie (*name the lie*). I desire to forgive (*person*) for (*the offense*). I've been made to feel (*share your emotions*). I now choose to give those toxic emotions to you to carry. Bring to my mind new images to change my anxious memory. In Jesus's name.

(Listen. What good news is coming to your mind?)

Respond: I receive that Lord.

Work-Steps: Update and Renew an EOM in 6-Steps

Read through the steps first, then write out your responses to each step. You will be coached through these 6-steps.

1. State your EOM as you remember it.
2. How has this memory affected your life in general?
3. How does this EOM make you feel emotionally?
4. When you believe this EOM, how does your body react?
5. Question and investigate the truth of the EOM.
6. Create a revised memory by adding a new positive experience to it.

Prepare your mind, brain, and body.

- Find your Jesus safe place; a place where you feel calm and grounded.
- Do some deep breathing until you feel ready and relaxed.
- Listen to your breathing. Don't try to slow or alter it.
- Breathe in God's goodness and love; breathe out any anxiety or fear.
- Do the eye movement exercises on page 73-74.

Step 1—State your EOM as you remember it.

Bring up an intrusive EOM which is disabling you from living in the present. Or ask God, *Is there a specific memory You want to heal?*

Pray, *God, what do I need to know about this memory, about myself or the event?*

Step 2—How has this memory affected your life in general?

Express as best you can the outcome and consequences of this event. What was the lie you believed because of this event?

Step 3—How does this EOM make you feel emotionally?

Use "The Feeling Wheel" in Appendix B to help you express yourself.

Step 4—When you believe this EOM, how does your body react?

- Does your body feel uncomfortable?
- Does the EOM cause your breathing to change (shorten, quicken, etc.)?
- What physical sensations arise (i.e., blood pressure rises, get nauseous, hands start to shake, headachy, experience insomnia)?
- Pray and ask Jesus to help you let go of the sensations.

Step 5—Question and investigate the truth of the EOM.

Answer to the best of your ability: *Can I be absolutely certain it's true?* Take the time to inquire, look for proof, and dig deeper. We want to look at reality instead of perceptions. Ask, "What are the facts? Am I looking at this all wrong?"

Step 6—Create revised memory by adding a new positive experience to it.

Think of 2 to 3 pieces of positive information you can use to restructure your reaction to the EOM. Example,

- Your memory makes you feel unsafe. Search your memory bank for a time that you did feel safe. For example, when you'd visit your grandma, or a teacher who helped you.
- If you can't think of an experience, search God's Word for promises that He is with you and protecting you.
- You can use visualization to create an image where you feel safe.
- Jot some key words down that express how this image makes you feel—emotionally, physically, and spiritually.
- Find the thought from the PTB list that goes with this new image.
- Attach God's Word—the truth—to the PTB and create a phrase that you can associate with it the memory such as, "God is good" or "God is great" or "God loves me so much."

Positive Experience	PTB	Scripture
Experience: Visiting Grandma	I'm not in danger any longer.	*Psalm 119:68* God is good and loving.

Or, God promises to be my Protector Or, In my mind I see myself interacting with a group of safe people.		
Overall feelings: Warm, comfortable, at ease.	I'm safe now.	*Psalm 32:7* God protects me.

Techniques to Help You Regulate Your Emotions

Feeling anxious about working on a particular EOM is normal. If all this seems overwhelming, these two exercises can help you regulate your thinking and emotions.

Distance Yourself from the EOM using the Window Technique

Envision a huge warehouse with lots of windows. You then walk up to one of the windows which is sealed off. You don't climb in; just look inside. There you see your memory; the incident. You are safe outside the window. You've separated yourself from all the emotions and feelings of it; it's sealed behind a window. You're merely observing the experience, along with your thoughts and emotions. Doing this can make the memory seem smaller and more manageable.

Third Person View

You can look at the memory and issue in the 3rd person—almost as if you're talking to someone else about the issue and advising them. Objectify the memory, which helps calm down the toxic stress reaction. Simply analyze it as an observer. You are distancing yourself from the issue which helps define its limitations, thereby you can move forward.

Work-Steps: Update and Renew Your EOM in 6-Steps

Step 1—State your EOM as you remember it.

—How does this EOM make you feel emotionally?

Step 4—When you believe this EOM, how does your body react?

Step 6—Create a revised memory by adding a new positive experience to it.

Positive Experience	PTB	Scripture
Experience:		
Overall feelings:		

Additional Therapeutic Tools
Keep a Trigger Log

Every one of us has different memory networks dealing with friends, family, school, work and church, for example. Different raw memories can get triggered depending upon the type of relationship and the situation. A *trigger* is when a file cabinet of memories is opened up, spilling out all the pleasantries or unpleasantries of a past event or events.

To move forward, we want to identify situations that trigger an inner disturbance. By using a Triggers Log, we can monitor our reactions.

- *Name the trigger.* Jot down a sentence or two that describes *your perception of the trigger event.*
- We want to answer the *who, what, where, when* and *whys.* What happened? Was it an argument, a look, a gesture, a smell, someone who made you feel less than? Who was with you? Where were you? What time of day did this happen? When do they happen most often? And how often?
- Is it happening with just one person, or a crowd, or with family, on the job, certain friends, strangers, alone?

- *Image.* What image comes to mind; the part that really upsets you, the part that makes you feel less than, or ashamed, or unworthy, for example. Briefly describe the image.
- *Choose the NTB* that best fits your feelings when you think of this event.
- What *emotions* are you feeling as you bring the image to mind?
- Where do you feel the tension/distress in your *body?*

This log can give you an opportunity to clarify where you need to put your focus. Using a Triggers Log will help you become more aware of what types of experiences and memories run your life. When we can figure out what and who triggers us, then we can choose to do something new and different. The log can help you mentally and physically prepare yourself before going into those kinds of situations.

Develop a Timeline

If you want a deeper perspective, you can start putting your memories in a timeline to further understand your own history. The purpose is to get a sense of when you developed different negative reactions, feelings, and beliefs. It can give you an idea of who added to those problems, and if there is any connection with any of the people that you're currently having difficulty with. Start with the youngest age.

One way is to create a different page for the different stages of life:

- Nursery: Years 1 to 5. (If you don't have any memories, this is normal.)
- Childhood: Years 5 to 10.
- Adolescence: Years 11 to 18.
- Early Adulthood: Years 11 to 25.
- Adulthood: Years 26 and over.

End of Session 4.

This Work Is Done!

As Mary Poppins said, "My work here is done." Actually, Jesus said it first! (John 17:4).

I'm so proud of you for persevering. It takes great courage to do The Work. It's been rough—okay, VERY rough, but your courage and faith in God got you through. No doubt, God has brought hope and healing into your life, and demolished some big strongholds. Your story and life have changed.

Share in Paul's joy, *"I have fought the good fight, I have finished the race, I have kept the faith" (2 Timothy 4:7).* We can stand up and bring God's light and love to the darkness and evil of this world—even the gates of hell will not be able to hold us back! (Matthew 16:18)

Many women ask, "Does healing ever end?" The answer is no. There's always some sort of memory and remnant of the wound that can still affect the mind and body; some kind of sensitivity and trigger, even if we've worked at reshaping it. But *the power* of that wound diminishes with healing and time. There's still scar tissue, but the wound doesn't run our lives anymore.

As broken, fallible humans living in a shattered world, we will be hurt in the future and a new race to heal will start. But, as we bring each wound to God, He will help us respond biblically to the thoughts, beliefs, feelings, and memories, rather than get trapped in them. *"He heals the brokenhearted and bandages their wounds"* (Psalm 147:3).

> *Let all that I am praise the LORD; with my whole heart, I will praise his holy name. Let all that I am praise the LORD; may I never forget the good things he does for me. He forgives all my sins and heals all my diseases. He redeems me from death and crowns me with love and tender mercies. He fills my life with good things. My youth is renewed like the eagle's!* (Psalm 103:1-5)

✝ ✝ ✝

For some people, regardless of how much information they have been given, old untreated memories get stuck in their network and won't budge. For a number of reasons, they haven't been able to link up with anything transformative.

If you didn't find any of these exercises helpful or healing, please seriously consider working with a licensed therapist.

11

Befriend and Pamper God's Temple

Take care of you! This last chapter is about pampering and nurturing your amazing body—"the temple" as the Bible calls it.

In America we spend billions of dollars sculpting, enhancing and perfecting our bodies and appearance. I too have spent my hard-earned dollars on hordes of empty promises.

The apostle Paul spoke of the physical body quite a bit.

Do you not know that your body is a temple of the Holy Spirit, who is in you, whom you have received from God? You are not your own; you were bought at a price. Therefore, honor God with your body" (1 Cor. 6:19-20).

In biblical times a temple was a sacred place, the house of God. The people believed that God dwelled in the temple. Paul knew that the human body had a wonderful origin and an even greater future; that the believer's body is actually part of Christ Himself. *"Do you not know that your bodies are members of Christ himself?"* (1 Corinthians 6:15)

Science has repeatedly documented that we are what we eat. The sum of all your experiences affects the health of your body. If you feed your body junk and convenience foods, it will simply lay down fat, lower your energy and brain power. If you're constantly in a stress mode it will do the same thing.

Think of your body as a finely tuned vehicle, a Maserati for example. We all have up to 100 trillion cells in our bodies, each one demanding a constant supply of daily nutrients in order to function optimally. Food affects all of these cells, and by extension, every aspect of our being: mood, energy levels, food cravings, thinking capacity, sex drive, sleeping habits and general health. Every 35 days your skin replaces itself, and your body makes new cells from the food you eat. What you eat *literally* becomes *you*.

Every believer should examine her life physically, emotionally, and relationally in light of how it affects the larger body of Christ. It reminds me of Jesus's ministry of purging His Father's house of unholy business practices (Matthew 21:12-13).

In a sense, we must do the same—strive to be honorable vessels, purging that which is untruthful and unholy out of our lives.

> *"Dear friend, I hope all is well with you and that you are as healthy in body as you are strong in spirit"* (3 John: 1:2); *I plead with you to give your bodies to God because of all he has done for you. Let them be a living and holy sacrifice—the kind he will find acceptable. This is truly the way to worship him"* (Romans 12:1). *I pray that God, who gives peace, will make you completely holy. And may your spirit, soul, and body be kept healthy and faultless until our Lord Jesus Christ returns.* (1 Thessalonians 5:23; CEV).

Overall well-being requires we engage in activities that help maintain proper functioning of our temples—our hearts, minds, bodies and spirits.

"Don't Worry, Be Happy"

> *Don't worry, be happy*
> *In every life we have some trouble*
> *But when you worry you make it double*
> *Don't worry, be happy; Don't worry, be happy now.*

Francis of Assisi said, "Let us leave sadness to the devil and his angels. As for us, what can we be but rejoicing and glad?" We can face adversity and still have joy. In the Bible, we see that, despite their circumstances, the people who follow God have joy and passion for life. Scripture states,

> *The people the LORD has freed will return and enter Jerusalem **with joy**. Their **happiness** will last forever. They will have **joy and gladness**, and all sadness and sorrow will be gone far away (Isaiah 51:11; NCV); For I have given rest to the weary and **joy to the sorrowing** (Jeremiah 31:25).*

One study stated that children laugh an average of 400 times a day; adults only 15 times.[49] What do you think happens between childhood and adulthood that damages our capacity for fun, laughter and happiness? Sadly, there's a segment of Christians who believe and tell other Christians that to pursue happiness is unrealistic and unbiblical. I can't tell you how many times I've heard people say God's desire is not to make us happy but to make us holy. I'm not disputing His objective is to make us holy. I'm disputing that His goal is to rip happiness from us in order to make us holy.

Comic Relief

A new monk arrives at the monastery. He is assigned to help the other monks in copying the old texts by hand. He notices, however, that they are copying copies, and not the original books. So, the new monk goes to the head monk to ask him about this. He points out that if there was an error in the first copy, that error would be continued in all of the other copies. The head monk says, "We've been copying from the copies for centuries, but you make a good point, my son."

So, he goes down into the cellar with one of the copies to check it against the original. Hours later, nobody has seen him. One of the monks goes downstairs to look for him. He hears sobbing coming from the cellar and finds the old monk leaning over one of the original books crying. He asks what's wrong.

"You idiots" he says, with anger and sadness in his eyes, "The word is celebrate, not celibate!"

It's been said the most wasted day is one in which we have not laughed. Did you know having a good laugh actually strengthens relationship bonds and makes for a stronger heart? Laughter, like water, flushes toxins out of our body. One study found that just 15 minutes of watching a funny movie *increased* average blood flow by 22%, while watching a serious drama or horror flick *decreased* blood flow by 35%.

When we laugh, we *diffuse pain*, like the pain of rejection, by physically increasing the body's production of endorphins (natural painkillers). Many professional comediennes found this out early in life. Humor became their defense mechanism against bullies and abusers and stress. Now I understand why I made "eye" jokes when I suddenly went blind in my left eye—to alleviate pain.

In the Old Testament, *"Sarah declared, 'God has brought me laughter. All who hear about this will laugh with me'"* (Genesis 21:6). Jesus frequently used humor and wit to make His point. Our response may be, "Really? Where?" Different cultures have different ways of being humorous. When we translate any language into another, we will often miss subtle nuances of speech. If we don't have a knowledge of the original language and its idioms, we can miss the humor.

Jesus used one form of humor we call sarcasm. In His responses to Herod, for example, He called him a fox. He made other statements that had a touch of humor to them, **like when He mentioned a camel going through the eye of a needle.** I can't imagine Jesus didn't laugh. Afterall, He was fully human. Since God has appointed times for laughter, it would seem to me that when it was time to laugh, He had a good belly laugh. **We all need to laugh more; have a good belly laugh**—even at ourselves.

God promises, *"He will once again fill your mouth with laughter and your lips with shouts of joy"* (Job 8:21). Is it time for you to laugh? Can you laugh at yourself when you've messed up?

Food, Nutrition and a Healthy Gut

I've been on a diet for 2 weeks and all I've lost is 2 weeks! –Totie Fields

Would it surprise you to know that malnutrition in America is a problem? We tend to eat too many "empty" calories and not enough nutrients. We overeat yet we're undernourished simply because we choose to eat more "dead" (processed) foods than "living" (fresh and raw) foods. Dead foods affect our quality of living—our mindset, mood and energy levels, as well as our mental and physical performance.

Many of us struggle with our relationship to food. For decades I battled with overeating and being compulsive with food. Food—it's our friend, our comforter, even our lover—it affects our psyche and physiology. If we feel bad, lots of us eat … and eat. Then we gain weight which makes us feel "yucky" and depressed … so we eat. For the abused, there is quite often a hidden psychological reason for eating more. In their minds added weight can protect them—from the abuser, bullies or other monsters. The term "comfort food" is literal.

If we are compulsive overeaters, we need to choose to dive deep and figure out the emotional whys, and find a healthier way to deal with our anxieties, stresses and memories. If we don't, what we find is the nasty downward spiral continues.

Sugar and Body Inflammation

Today the average American consumes around 160 pounds of sugar per person, per year. (That doesn't include high fructose corn sugar.) Sugar is in almost everything we eat. Just read the ingredient labels. Consider that one of those "healthy" fruit yogurt cups or bottle of "real" fruit juice is loaded with sugar.

There are consequences: Weight gain and obesity, diabetes (insulin resistance) and certain types of cancer. Sugar increases our triglycerides (fat levels) in the blood, and higher triglycerides increase the risk for heart disease.

Too much sugar can cause chronic low-grade inflammation in the body. *Inflammation* is a primary cause of most lifestyle related disorders, including heart disease and musculoskeletal disorders. It is invisible and subtle. It's on our inside and we don't necessarily feel it—but it's a fire within the body that is slowly burning our soft tissues from the inside out. Our entire body can be in an inflamed state. [50]

For example, one study found that healthy people who consumed only 40 grams of added sugar (1 can of soda) per day, had an increase in inflammatory markers, insulin resistance, LDL cholesterol. Eating just 50 grams of refined carbs in the form of white bread resulted in higher sugar levels and an increase in inflammatory markers.[51]

Inflammation looks for small cracks or vulnerabilities in the body and then attacks those weaknesses. Taking an anti-inflammatory drug may seem like it would fix the problem but it doesn't address the cause. The biggest cause of this fire in our bodies is caused by sugars and fats from our diets. Other factors are stress, lack of exercise, and food allergies, and sensitivities.

A healthy diet is one of the best weapons we have to fight against chronic physical and mental illness. Experts say that just cutting out processed sugar can reduce the ups and downs of mood and energy, important for happiness and health.

When I changed my diet to more "living" foods my high blood sugar and cholesterol decreased, and my adrenal glands performed better. I have more energy. Eating well is a process, not a one-time-event. It's a lifestyle and lifetime change. Setbacks do happen so give yourself grace.

The Good Gut

It's all the talk now—gut health. Why is gut health so important for our bodies and our minds?

You've probably heard these two terms—*probiotics* and *prebiotics*—are becoming more widely known. Probiotics are beneficial good gut bugs. And prebiotics are food for these bacteria—which we get by eating the right foods.

The gut is composed of a whole host of microbes that affect our physiology and keep our bodies and brain functioning as they should. Researchers have identified almost 2,000 new gut bacteria. As studies tell us, these gut microbes affect the way we store fat, balance levels of glucose in our blood, and how we respond to hormones that make you feel hungry or satiated. The wrong internal mix can set the stage for obesity and other health issues later in life.

Positive bacteria we ingest are often called healthy "gut bugs." Good gut bugs help our body digest and absorb nutrients, synthesize certain vitamins, and rally against intruders, such as the flu and toxic-forming carcinogens which translates into a healthy human.

So how can we keep our digestive system feeling good and functioning optimally? What are the best foods for gut health? Think fiber, fermentation, greens, fruits, and nutrient-dense foods.

The good news is, *even a lifetime of bad eating is fixable*—at least as far as your microbes are concerned. Amazingly, your body can create a new microorganism in as little as 24 hours, just by changing what you eat.

What you eat determines which kinds of bacteria thrive in your gut. And research tells us that the good "gut bugs" get stronger when fed colorful, plant-based foods. A recognized 2014 study published in the journal *The Proceedings of the Nutrition Society* found that vegetables, grains, and beans fed a positive gut environment. On the other hand, meat, processed food, dairy, gluten, and eggs fed a negative gut environment.

Ouch! I love dairy, eggs and meat! However, many nutrition experts say to include lean meats, dairy, and eggs in the diet. The protein balances blood sugar. As they say, "Everything in moderation." That's my moto!

Eating for Mental Health

Food is medicine—for the body and mind. Scientists report that a healthy well-balanced diet reduces autoimmune disease, depression and anxiety, psoriasis and other disease symptoms.

Daniel G. Amen, M.D., is a Christian clinical neuroscientist, psychiatrist, and brain-imaging expert who heads up the world-renowned Amen Clinics. He is a Distinguished Fellow of the American Psychiatric Association and has won numerous research awards. He is considered an expert on the brain and eating for physical and mental health. He writes,

> Your brain is the most energy-hungry organ in your body. 20 to 30% of the calories you consume go directly to your brain. If you eat a fast-food diet, you can expect to have a fast-food mind that is less capable of thinking clearly. On the other hand, supplying your body with fruits, vegetables, and lean protein boosts your brain's functionality. First Corinthians 10:31 says, *"whether you eat or drink or whatever you do, do it all for the glory of God."* To keep your memory and spiritual life healthy, it is important to focus on eating brain-healthy food.[52]

The American Cancer Society recommends 5 to 9 servings of fruits and vegetables a day. (I know, that's a lot!) Mixing colors—eating from the rainbow—is a good way to think about healthy fruits and vegetables. Strive to eat *red foods* (strawberries, beets, raspberries, cherries, red peppers and tomatoes), *yellow foods* (squash, yellow peppers, cauliflower, small portions of bananas and peaches), *blue foods* (blueberries), *purple foods* (plums), *orange foods* (oranges, tangerines and yams), *green foods* (peas, spinach and broccoli). And eat slow because the brain needs 20-minutes to register that we are full.

Dr. Amen has listed some brain-promoting nutritional tips to get our diet under control and to use food as brain medicine. (Copyright © 2005 Daniel G. Amen, M.D.)

Calorie restriction: Substantial research in animals and now in humans indicates that a calorie-restricted diet is helpful for brain and life longevity. Eating less helps you live longer. It controls weight; decreases risk for heart disease, cancer, and stroke from obesity (a major risk factor for all of these illnesses); and it triggers certain mechanisms in the body to increase the production of nerve growth factors, which are helpful to the brain. Researchers use the acronym CRON for "Calorie Restriction with Optimal Nutrition." In other words: Make your calories count.

Fish and Fish Oils: DHA, one form of omega-3 fatty acids found in fish, makes up a large portion of the gray matter of the brain. The fat in your brain forms cell membranes and plays a vital role in how our cells function. Neurons are also rich in omega-3 fatty acids. DHA is also found in high quantities in the retina, the light-sensitive part of the eye. Research in the last few years has revealed that diets rich in omega-3 fatty acids may help promote a healthy emotional balance and positive mood in later years, possibly because DHA is a main component of the brain's synapses.

Dietary Antioxidants: A number of studies have shown that dietary intake of antioxidants from fruits and vegetables significantly reduce the risk of developing cognitive impairment. The research was done because it was theorized that free radical formation plays a major role in the deterioration of the brain with age. When a cell converts oxygen into energy, tiny molecules called free radicals are made. When produced in normal amounts, free radicals work to rid the body of harmful toxins, thereby keeping it healthy. When produced in toxic amounts, free radicals damage the body's cellular machinery, resulting in cell death and tissue damage.

This process is called *oxidative stress*. Vitamin E and Vitamin C and beta carotene inhibit the production of free radicals. The best antioxidant fruits and vegetables are blueberries, blackberries, cranberries, strawberries, spinach, raspberries, brussels sprouts, plums, broccoli, beets, avocados, oranges, red grapes, red bell peppers, cherries and kiwis.

Balance Protein, Good Fats and Carbohydrates: Balance is essential, especially balancing proteins, good fats, and good carbohydrates. Having protein at each meal helps to balance blood sugar levels; adding lean meat, eggs, cheese, soy, or nuts to a snack or meal limits the fast absorption of carbohydrates and prevents the brain fog that goes with eating simple "empty" carbohydrates, such as donuts. At each meal or snack, try to get a balance of protein, high fiber carbohydrates and fat.

Lean Protein
- Fish: Salmon (especially Alaskan Salmon caught in the wild, farmed fish is not as rich in omega-3-fatty acids), tuna, mackerel, herring (also listed under fats)
- Poultry: skinless chicken and turkey
- Meat: lean beef and pork
- Eggs (enriched DHA eggs are best)
- Tofu and soy products (whenever possible choose organically raised)
- Dairy products: low fat cheeses and cottage cheese, low fat sugar free yogurt and low fat or skim milk
- Beans, especially garbanzo beans and lentils (also listed under carbohydrates)
- Nuts and seeds, especially walnuts (also listed under fats). Great recipe: soak walnuts in water and sea salt overnight, drain and sprinkle with cinnamon (natural blood sugar balancer) and low roast 4 hours at 250 degrees. This makes them easier to digest.

Complex Carbohydrates
- Berries: blueberries (called "brain berries"), raspberries, strawberries, blackberries
- Oranges, lemons, limes, grapefruit
- Cherries and peaches, plums
- Broccoli, cauliflower, Brussels sprouts

- Oats, whole wheat, wheat germ: oatmeal needs to be the long cooking kind as instant has a higher glycemic index since the manufacturer has broken down the fiber to speed cooking time and basically make it a refined carbohydrate. With bread, look for at least 3 grams of fiber. Remember unbleached wheat flour is white flour, it must say whole wheat.
- Red or yellow peppers (much higher in Vitamin C than green peppers)
- Pumpkin squash
- Spinach, tomatoes and yams
- Beans (also listed under proteins)

Fats: Extra virgin olive oil, coconut and avocado oil; Salmon (also listed under protein); Nuts and nut butter, especially walnuts, macadamia nuts, Brazil nuts, pecans and almonds (also listed under protein)

Tea: Green or black tea. Green tea is good for brain function as it contains chemicals that enhance mental relaxation and alertness.

Water (God's nectar)

Did you know *water is the most important non-food for your body?* Given that the brain is about 80% water, the first rule of brain nutrition is to drink enough water to hydrate your brain. Even slight dehydration can raise stress hormones which can damage your brain over time.

Our bodies cannot thrive without an adequate supply of water. It is the nutrient transportation system to the body and the brain. It aids in fat metabolism, helps concentration, alertness and muscle tone. It improves mood, regulates blood pressure, detoxifies and decreases water retention.[53] We need to drink lots of it for optimum function of all body systems.

If the body becomes dehydrated, the capability of the transport system is comprised. We lose strength and energy. Lack of water can produce metabolic waste and by-products like lactic acid, uric acid, ammonia and other toxins that accumulate in our soft tissues. Drinking adequate amounts of water throughout the day ensures that all this junk is properly flushed out.

The question most asked is: How much water should I drink? The standard answer used to be 6 to 8 glasses (8 ounces) a day, which is still not disputed. Yet, many nutritional experts state we need to take our body weight and divide it by two and drink that many ounces each day.

I weigh 130 pounds which means I must drink at least 65 ounces a day, which is 8 cups a day. So, if you weigh more than this you will need to drink more water. You can get *some* of your water also from fruits, sparkling water, even decaffeinated coffee (so I read).

Sleep

Jesus said, *"Let's go off by ourselves to a quiet place and rest awhile"* (Mark 6:31).

Our culture minimizes the importance of sleep. *I'm too busy to sleep.* Have you considered the effects of sleep deprivation? Decreased performance and fatigue, impaired memory, high blood pressure, heart failure, decreased quality of life, and the list goes on.

Sleep deprivation accumulates. Studies indicate that mortality increases with only 4 to 5 hours of nightly sleep. A short nap during the day may be appealing, however, that deep REM (rapid eye movement) and delta sleep (our deepest sleep) is what our bodies need for healing and recovery.

If we are sleep deprived our metabolic rate will slow down to conserve energy which is why we gain weight—we crave "comfort" and "dead" foods when we're sleepy.[54] Research has shown that insufficient sleep appears to tip hunger hormones out of whack. There is a link between sleeplessness and obesity. I know when I'm sleep deprived, I crave and gorge on carbs!

Our immune system suffers too. There is a lot of data showing that a good night's sleep stabilizes, heals the body (muscles and tissues at a cellular level), strengthens, and integrates our memories. It gives our brain a chance to regroup and consolidate information.

Lack of sleep makes you cranky! And have you noticed when we're cranky we're less cute? ☺Researchers also found the language center shuts down in the brains of healthy young people who took a simple word test after staying awake 35 hours.[55] This explains why I have mush-mouth when I'm sleep deprived!

Sleep helps the mind, brain, and body regenerate. When you go to sleep, you are kind of going into a "housekeeping" mode—everything is cleaned up, which helps prepare you for the next day. We need to make sure we get enough sleep to allow this regeneration to happen. This will be different for everyone, as we all have different schedules, lifestyles and needs—the average amount of sleep an adult should get is 6 to 8 hours.

We also need to look at the context of our life: what we are eating, any medications we are taking, our emotional state is, our work schedule, our thought life and so on. These will all affect the quality of our sleep, and how much we sleep. Consider that sleep is anything but a state of inactivity. Our bodies may be still but our brains are busy at work. Getting enough sleep leads to better learning and memory; it facilitates healing and reduces levels of inflammatory markers in the body.

Appropriate Touch

Did you know that *proper* touch accelerates the healing process because it has positive benefits to the immune system? It's true. It also can alleviate psychosomatic (mind—body) illness. This is why "touch therapy" for many people is a recognized modality.

When was the last time you touched someone in a non-sexual way? Maybe you held and petted your kitten, or hugged your friend when you said hi, or you had a good cuddle before getting out of bed this morning.

Touch is one of those things that we don't usually think about actively, but it's really important for our health and happiness. That's because it not only feels great but also boosts levels of *oxytocin*, which is a key hormone for love, happiness and bonding. Despite the benefits, most of us aren't getting enough non-sexual intimate touch.

Accepting healthy physical touch can be a challenge if all we've known is toxic touch. When physical touch is harming versus nurturing, a person's soul is endangered. It will take time, mind renewal, and often counseling, to restore a sense of trust when it comes to healthy touch.

Mend the Body by Moving the Body

I think everyone knows by now that a sedentary lifestyle is bad for our health and that regular exercise is good for it. It is proven to reduce the risk of depression, heart disease; lower blood pressure, reduce pain, improve sleep, enhance energy, lose or maintain a healthy body weight; it slows brain shrinkage, builds strength and lowers stress. Millions of Americans suffer from all kinds of illnesses that could be prevented through improved diet and physical activity.

We know body fat is bad for our overall health (obesity lops off as much as 20 years of life), but did you know it's bad for your brain? One study explained that too much sitting harms the *temporal lobe*, an area of the brain that plays an essential role in processing memories and language. Exercise helps to sharpen thinking by oxygenating the brain and optimizing mental performance.

One study in *Medical News Today* showed that aerobic exercise helps preserve brain health, keeping neurodegenerative diseases, such as dementia, at bay. Research from Kaiser Permanente found those with the fattest arms at ages 40 to 45 were 59% likely to have dementia later in life. Another study found those with particularly large bellies at midlife, were 260% more likely to develop dementia.[56]

Experts say we should incorporate three types of exercise into our wellness plan: aerobic or cardiovascular, strength training and stretching or flexibility exercise.

This always bears repeating: *Regular activity can improve your quality of life—physical, mental and spiritual.* Period.

Serve Others

Self-examination and doing The Work is an act of self-care, which is anything but selfish because the better we feel, the more we can give to others. God calls Christians to all kinds of work for Him.

N. T. Wright said, "The work of salvation is about what God does through us, not merely what God does in and for us." "*God has created us anew in Christ Jesus, so we can do the good things he planned for us long ago*"

(Ephesians 2:10). "Good things" may involve doing world-changing missions; most often, the work is much more personal and closer to home.

Secondly, focusing on others can distract us from our own distress and give us a sense of mission, meaning, and purpose. It can release oxytocin and dopamine, and lower activity in our stress response system.

The Bible gives us *numerous* commands to help and serve others; to use our unique spiritual gifts. When the Spirit works through surrendered, faith-filled people, God is glorified and the Church gets stronger. Helping others not only makes God and us happier, it's contagious!

Engage in the Real World

Technology can be highly addictive and have negative effects on our overall well-being. Enough said; we've all heard the lecture!

Bible Study

What place does Bible study hold in your life? All of us should be concerned to study God's Word, for in doing so we will be able to **get to know God better, we can reframe our error-based perspectives and alter our image brain maps,** as well as present a Christian worldview to those in our circle. **Never forget that God's plan is perfect and His perspective is absolutely "flawless" as Psalm 18:30 says.** *"Your word is a lamp to guide my feet and a light for my path"* *(Psalm 119:105).*

It's helpful to have several good translations of the Bible to compare with each other which you can get through Bible apps or online. Doing so adds insight. For example, in the New King James Version (NKJV), 2 Timothy 1:7 says God has given us a spirit *"of power and of love and of a sound mind."* But the New International Version (NIV) says, *"power, love and self-discipline."* Strive to make Bible study a regular part of your life.

Appendix A

Glossary of Terms

- *ACE:* Adverse Childhood Experience (Kimberly's story: Awesome Christ Experience)

- *BASK:* Behavior; Affect (emotions); Sensation (physical); Knowledge

- *NTB:* Negative Thinking Beliefs

- *Neuroplastic:* Our brains are changeable throughout life. *Neuro* = brain cells; *Plastic* = changed and altered.

- *Processed Memory:* Identifying specific NTBs and memories that need to be treated, then doing The Work.

- *PTB:* Positive Thought and Belief

- *PTSD:* Post-traumatic Stress Disorder and Present-traumatic Stress Disorder

- *PTSI:* Post-traumatic Stress Injury

- *PAG:* Post-Adversive Growth

- *SUD:* Subjective Units of Distress rating system.

The Feeling Wheel

Identified or labeled feelings are manageable; unidentified emotions can feel overwhelming. Use this chart to identify exactly how you feel. Ask Jesus to help you clarify your feelings.

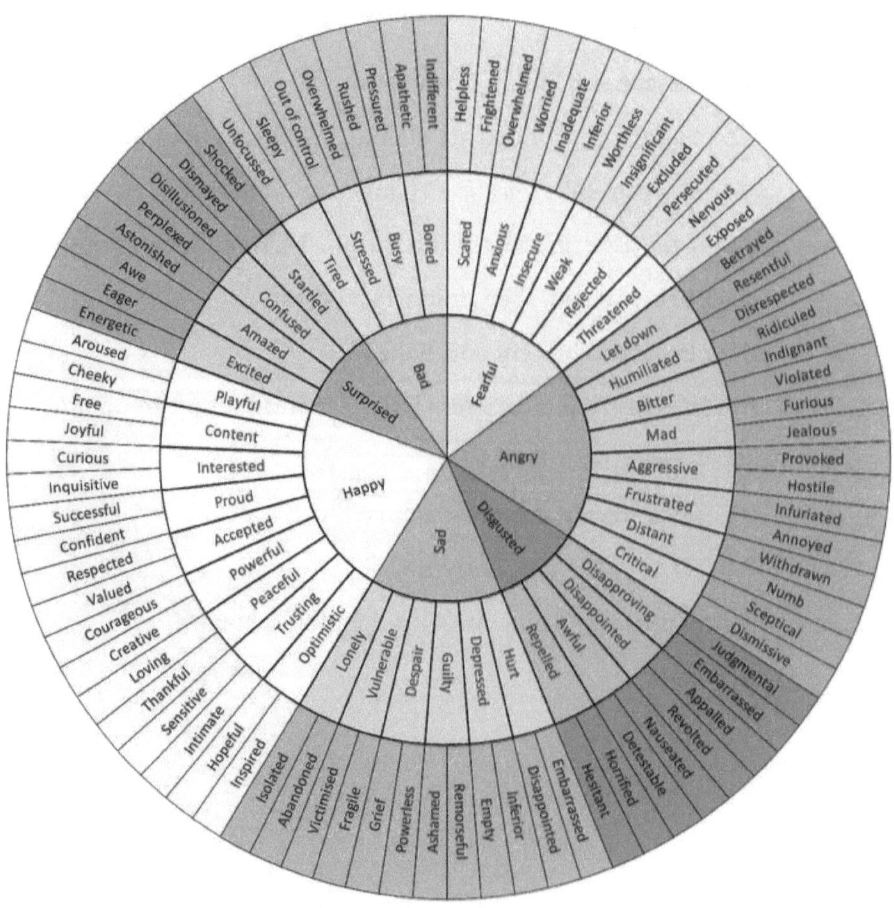

The Brain

Cerebrum
Parietal Lobe
Frontal Lobe
Temporal Lobe
Midbrain
Brainstem
Pons
Medulla
Occipital Lobe
Cerebellum
Parietal Lobes
Occipital Lobes
Cerebellum
Left Hemisphere
Right Hemisphere
Cerebrocerebellum
Spinocerebellum
Vestibulocerebellum

A PICTURE OF GOOD HEALTH

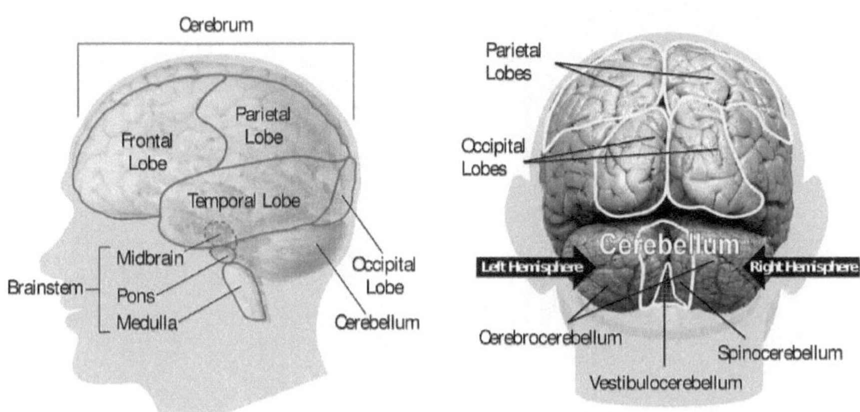

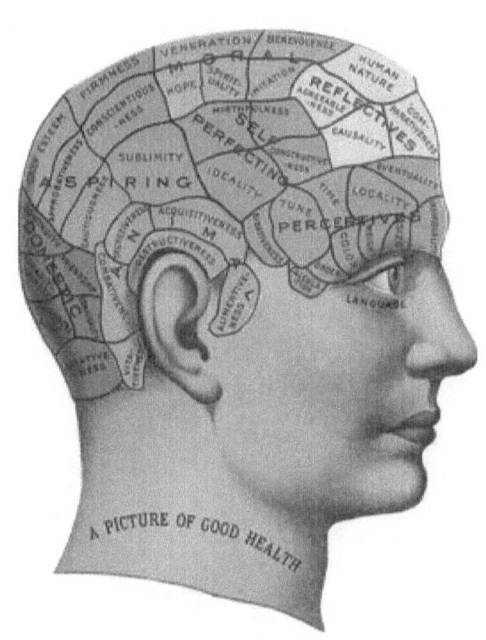

About the Author | Kimberly's Story

Kimberly Davidson lived two decades of her life in complete turmoil; in pain and addiction. Jesus heard the cry of her heart. He saw her pain and interceded, freeing her in 1989 from her personal prison. Today she calls herself a "wounded healer." She uses her voice, life wisdom from doing her own work, and pen to write curriculum and books for women in pain.

Kimberly is a board-certified biblical counselor, helping women mend their souls. She received her MA in specialized ministry from Western Seminary, Portland, Oregon; a BA in health sciences from the University of Iowa. She considers herself a lifelong learner. Kimberly has ministered to women for over 15-years, from within prison walls to youth centers, inspiring others to empower God to meet their emotional and spiritual needs.

She created *Olive Branch Outreach*, an interactive website dedicated to bring hope and restoration to those struggling with body image, abuse and food addiction. In addition, Kimberly leads an abuse recovery program at a federal women's prison. She is also a consultant of abuse education and recovery for *Freedom Calling*, an anti-sex trafficking a ministry; and is a contributor to *Living in Truth*, a ministry that helps women who struggle with unhealthy eating and body image. She lives in Oregon on a small ranch with her husband and many critters.

If you want to connect with Kimberly, you can through her website at *OliveBranchOutreach.com* or on *Facebook*. Or, email her at *kim@kim-davidson.com*.

Kimberly's Story

If you saw me walking down the street in my 20s, 30s and 40s, you'd have seen a well-dressed blonde-haired blue-eyed woman who displayed a sense of confidence and competency, like she had it all together. What you saw on the outside was far from reality.

On the surface my childhood seems "normal." I had two healthy parents who stayed married through thick and thin. We lived in nice middle-class neighborhoods. Dad worked very hard to advance his career. (Unfortunately, the cost of being professionally successful is that a busy schedule leads to neglect of family life.) Mom stayed at home with me and my two younger brothers. It appeared we had an ideal family, particularly because never once did I hear my parents fight in their entire marriage, which now I know is a sign of a dysfunctional relationship. Sadly, my parents didn't create a safe space where us children could feel free to express our feelings and be our real selves.

Childhood Adversity

As a kid, our family moved quite a bit. The first major move was when I was 7-years-old, moving from Iowa to London, England. When you're that young, you don't have an opinion about moving. You submit and go.

Nothing was normal anymore. In London, schoolmates teased me because I didn't fit into their culture. I wasn't like them because I had an accent. *Weird kid from America,* they'd chant. No one wanted me in their groups or on their teams, leaving me alone and devastated.

I felt stupid because I needed a math tutor. To them I was odd because my clothes were different. I remember going through a time of pulling out my hair, strand by strand, a way to cope with the stress. I had a tendency to be the mean girl. I wanted my "targets" to feel as bad as I did.

I'll never forget my first gym class. Unbeknownst to our family, the boys and girls had gym together. Each child was dressed in uniform underwear—dark navy-blue "knickers" (English for *underpants*) and a thick, stark white undershirt. I slithered into the gym wearing a flimsy undershirt with a cute little bow and worn out, flowery panties with a big hole along the elastic line! The kids laughed and pointed at me.

Please daddy, can we go back to America?

These memories were imprinted and activated each time I was rejected by a peer, particularly during my school years. You never get used to other kids being mean, but in time you learn how not to feel the sting of rejection so much because of a deep-seeded need for acceptance.

I worked tirelessly to conform to the way I thought my peer group and teachers wanted me to be. Feeling a great deal of pressure from the culture, I lost my real identity and created a false self—a Cover Girl mask.

When I think back to living in Iowa, I have "warm" memories; compared to having "cold" memories of the first years in London.

The Second Move

We moved back to America when I was 12-years-old. Even though I finally integrated into the English culture, I looked forward to moving back to America. Sadly, *again,* I was considered weird and different in my classmates' eyes. Some boys nicknamed me Bozo, after the clown.

Now I was entering adolescence, the hurricane years. Further rejection and teasing from schoolmates only made the previous strongholds of shame and fear deeper—that feeling of being excluded, disregarded, unwanted, and cast out. The pain of rejection became part of my normal thought process. Unbeknownst to me, I was holding in a lot of emotional pain. (Rejection literally feels like pain to the brain.[57])

We moved several more times. Being a teen with strong opinions about "my life," I strongly objected, which made no difference to my parents. I had no voice in my family. It was "dad's way or the highway." For us kids, moving caused a lack of control over what was transpiring. The loneliness and loss of my few close friendships were injuries to my soul.

(40 million Americans move and relocate each year. The uprooted family, or person, is cut off from stabilizing deep-rooted relationships; their sense of belonging is torn away. Each person is adversely affected as they're pulled from people and things which they have grown to love. The fear of the unknown, finding a new home, friends, schools, is a major upheaval. Research shows relocating can affect the body's immune system. Psychologists agree that moving to a new school for many kids is the equivalent to dealing with a death in the family. Many are at risk for depression. Moving increases the risk of teen sexual activity; it's their way of gaining social acceptance. What can also happen is the kid unconsciously chooses to control a particular area of their life, like weight and food, snowballing into a destructive behavior or activity.[58])

Mom found a couple of my report cards from junior high school and sent them to me. Who flunks classes in junior high? I can see from these reports the agony I must have been in since I come from a long line of very intelligent people.

Feeling the pressure to fit in, I fell in with the wild crowd; my "gang." I shoplifted, smoked cigarettes, and tried alcohol and drugs. This group, and the substances, gave me false courage to override my flailing emotions.

I'll never forget the first time I got drunk in 8th grade. My best friend Liz and I got invited to a party at our friend Robin's house. We all agreed to steal alcohol from our parents and bring it to the party. I found an empty Flintstone jelly jar and filled it with Johnny Walker scotch. What an image!

Liz and I lied to our parents, telling them Robin invited us to spend the night. The plan was to camp out with our boyfriends. We got ripped. Then I fell, face first, on a gravel road, chipping my two front teeth and cutting up my entire upper lip. *Super ouch!* We stuck to the plan and camped out; we had no other choice.

Back then, junior high schoolers didn't hook up or have sex like today. "Hickeys" were the outward sign you had been intimate with your boyfriend. This was my first real boyfriend, and he covered my entire neck with his love language.

In the morning, filled with fear, I reluctantly called Dad from the campout location. "Pick me up at Robin's in 20-minutes," I whimpered. Dad got there early. When I wasn't there, he high-tailed it straight over to Liz's, who had confessed the night's activities to her mom. Now Dad knew *almost* everything.

He drove back to Robin's only to find his princess standing in the driveway in an unrecognizable state.

"What happened to you? Get in the car!"

He thought I'd been attacked.

I lied. "I fell down the stairs, and some kids pulled me up by my neck."

He already knew we'd been drinking alcohol. Punishment was unavoidable. Yet my parents told me they still loved me. I clearly remember those words because it's the only time I ever recall them telling me they loved me.

School on Monday morning wasn't much better. A young male teacher only rubbed salt in the wound when he called me "Hickey Hansen" (my maiden name) in front of the entire class. I wanted to run and hide. The shame kept piling on. However, these "wild" groups gave me a sense of belonging and a means to forget the distress and losses.

As I got closer to high school, I began to gravitate into a new world of worshipping celebrities and models. I believed the lie that to be accepted and popular you have to look like a model. Teen magazines whispered in my ears, *Don't worry about being good; worry about looking good and being socially accepted!*

I pretty much turned off my God-given talents and gifts in search of the Western culture's definition of the ideal. I decided I wanted a career as a super model and told some kids. Some boys laughed, "You'll be a model for *MAD Magazine.*"

The result: I entered into my own hell, crashing and burning as I navigated through social and physical development. I sold my soul for popularity, which I never completely received.

At this time in my life I never knew Jesus, and certainly never recognized that the evil one, Satan, was real. I didn't know he was the one murmuring to me, *You're ugly girlfriend. Give it up!* I didn't give it up. I'd do anything to be a super model or celebrity. And why not? In this culture beauty and celebrity has its rewards.

To me, all seemed "fine" despite the fact I didn't have an intimate relationship with my mom or dad. I could never express myself, and more importantly, they never asked me how I felt.

High School

Fast forward to my senior year in high school. In counseling there's a saying that goes something like this, "The gun was already loaded and cocked (referring to a genetic predisposition); then one day a bad experience squeezes the trigger—and all hell breaks loose." This particular experience I believe squeezed the trigger.

During dinner one evening, my dad snatched a plate of food away from me as I reached for seconds. He barked, "You can't have that—you're fat!" A typical rebellious teen, I grabbed the plate, made a defiant face at him, then scooped out a large serving of mashed potatoes.

"Get on the scale. I bet you weigh 150 pounds!" he growled.

If my dad thinks I'm fat, then everyone else does.

Despite my rebellious attitude, he never had a clue how crushing his remarks were. Decades later when I had an opportunity to express how this incident made me feel, he responded, "Isn't it interesting how the father always gets the blame!" (Mother-blaming is also rampant in our culture.)

Mid-senior year I decided to lose weight. What started as a diet ended up being a near 20-year battle with bulimia and other self-destructive behaviors. I abused substances like alcohol, cigarettes, diet pills, diuretics, and laxatives. I truly believed, *If I'm thinner, life will be perfect. I'll be a success, get a husband ... and Dad will be proud of me.*

Since those dark days I've learned that when you live under the control of a verbally abusive parent, you subconsciously rebel. No doubt my dad loved me, but he'd give out more put-downs than affirmations, making me feel incredibly small. I learned not to violate the unspoken family rules: *Do not acknowledge my own personal problems. Do not open up to mother or father. Do not give voice to my authentic self. Don't be real; be ideal.*

Adult Adversity

For 16 years you'd find me hanging out with my best friend, "Ed," my Eating disorder. It was my way to detach emotionally from my self-hatred and crappy life by bingeing, then purging. No doubt, the combination of adverse childhood events, combined with feelings of unworthiness, fear and loneliness, triggered the eating disorder. Ed, my defense mechanism, became a beneficial ally protecting me from the fear, loss and emotional pain.

College was a lot more difficult than I anticipated. I was afraid to fail and I desperately wanted to find a husband. To be honest, my only desire to attend college was to get my MRS degree—which I failed to receive. I did eventually get my bachelor's degree.

Fast-forward to my 20's and 30's. Most nights when I'd get home from work, I'd consume an inordinate amount of food. It's what I wanted; it's what I needed. An empty place filled ... a place I could numb out and forget the pain—only to be wakened up to sheer panic, *I've got to get it all out!* So, I'd purge the food, even if it meant scraping and bloodying up my throat.

My *conscious* mind said I had to get out every morsel of food—of fat—out. My *subconscious* said to get out every bad thought and feeling; every bad memory had to be flushed down the toilet.

My goal was to be skinny, a thin size 2—because if I was thin, I reasoned, I'd be in a better position to attract Prince Charming who would swoop in and take me away from my crappy life and pain.

Each morning, I'd wake up ready to start my diet ritual of counting calories and swore I wouldn't binge or purge. It felt good to be in control once more ... until my self-control got strained by the intensive impulse to eat a lot of scrumptious foods. I felt my mind being stretched to a breaking point by forces pulling in opposite directions. There was a tug-o-war going on between the little angel on one shoulder and the devil on the other.

I never could stay on my carefully planned restricted diet for the day. Resisting the desire to binge became a growing source of anxiety, that could only be put out by repeating the gruesome act. This self-destructive ritual controlled over 16-years of my life.

Satan, the "god of this world" (2 Corinthians 4:4), disguised himself as Ed just as he disguised himself as a serpent to Adam and Eve. He stole my dignity, expectations and dreams. He lied endlessly, and over time, destroyed my body. It was a "fatal attraction" — *I can't live with Ed; I can't live without him.*

My deceived mind believed my god Ed had been helping me, not hurting me, because Ed was really good at reframing pain and sin. This explains why I'd sabotage friendships. I'd been the type of girlfriend who dumped you as soon as a guy came along. Men and Ed became more important than valuable and needed friendships.

What I didn't know then is Ed was a coverup for something else. Bingeing was way more than eating comfort food because I had a stressful day at work. I had a deep emotional hunger for something else. My "head" goal was always to lose weight and be skinny—whereas my *soul's real objective* was to find God, love and acceptance.

I gave into another demon—alcohol, "Ed's drinking buddy." I convinced myself I was just a social drinker, only interested in having fun—and finding a husband. Drunk, I'd willingly give my body to guys who threw me away. My lack of self-worth was the very thing a guy quickly manipulated.

One of the many consequences of promiscuity was getting pregnant. Dealing with the unbearable, I justified abortion. I also got picked up for shoplifting, got a DUI and went to jail, and got fired from numerous jobs. An immature adult with the emotions of a child, the pain and shame and guilt just kept accumulating.

Looking for Love in all the Wrong Places

When a person's loneliness becomes too heavy, she may seek an unrealistic, and often dangerous, "hook-up." My weekends as a young adult were spent in bars looking for Mr. Right, followed by nursing hangovers and my dignity. I cannot count how many times I woke up with a strange man, staring at the ceiling, pretending to be loved and needed and desired.

Will he want to get to know me; perhaps ask me to spend the day with him? Or is he simply another "smooth operator?" Will he, like the others, promise to call only to dismiss me? Might he actually want to start a relationship—a meaningful love relationship my soul craves?

Then my mind switched tracks. Being repeatedly rejected in the past fueled cynical and destructive feelings: *I can't believe I'm in this place again. I feel used, abused, and embarrassed. I hate myself. This keeps happening because I'm bad.*

How many of us have looked for love in all the wrong places? Even when one's idealized fantasy rescuer becomes harsh or sarcastic or rude or abusive, we're oblivious to the signs and consequently become ensnared in a toxic relationship because it's so familiar—it's like "family."

What I also find interesting is that we get into relationships we don't truly want to be in, but the acceptance factor is so great. We jump through hoop after hoop to be accepted and loved. We don't know what it's like to be loved unconditionally with no strings attached. Our desire for touch and intimacy is so great we often delude ourselves into thinking sex will motivate a guy to "be there" for us.

I always had to have a man in my life. It was a kind of validation I wasn't as worthless as I felt I was. I believed, like so many women, that any kind of relationship is better than no relationship. *It's better to settle for crumbs.*

A New Life

The day came in 1989 when I couldn't take it any longer. I cried out to God. He sent me a man named Dennis who took me to an evangelical church. It felt awkward at first. As a child, I attended the Episcopal Church but was never introduced to Jesus as my personal Savior.

One night, Dennis (who is now my husband) encouraged me to watch Billy Graham on TV. I watched it. When Billy gave the call to accept Jesus as Lord and Savior at the end of the program, I accepted. Shortly after, miraculously my eating disorder—the urge to binge and purge numerous times a day—ended. I had been healed by the power of God alone. To quote Daniel 3:27 and 29: "*... for no other god can save this way.*"

My past flashed through my mind and I felt God saying,

"I saved you from that ..."
"I kept you from that ..."
"I watched over you there ..."
"I sent my angels there ..."

I waited patiently for the LORD; he turned to me and heard my cry. He lifted me out of the slimy pit, out of the mud and mire; he set my feet on a rock and gave me a firm place to stand (Psalm 40:1).

When I envision my "salvation day," I see a person charged with crimes of theft, drunkenness, pride, envy, covetousness and more. Jesus came into the courthouse and took care of my charges; He expunged them. With the most awesome grace, He looked into my broken soul and basically said, "Your Father will never know. And when He looks at you, He'll only see My perfection" (Romans 3:22). Wow!

Unfortunately, as a new Christian, I didn't see the Lord's hand. *"It is I* [God] *who took them in My arms; But they did not know that I healed them. I led them with bonds of love ..."* (Hosea 11:3-4; NASB).

Just like the Israelites, "I didn't know that Love had intervened in my life."

Nothing much changed because I remained a slave to other things. I went to church on Sunday's only and never fed myself the Word of God. I did watch the 700 club a couple times a week. But I kept slipping and falling.

Then 9/11 happened (2001), which turned out to be my wake-up call. I recommitted my life to Jesus and never turned back. This time I truly felt transformed into a "new creation" (2 Corinthians 5:17) which means I was no longer the same person; I became made new spiritually by the power of God.

My old life was over; a new life begun!" I got a life do-over. For me that meant my "reputation" disappeared as Jesus changed my identity. In time, my emotions and relationships followed. God became a very real and living presence in my life.

Thankfully, He pursues us even when we're disobedient! Yet, I couldn't help wondering, *Who would I have been? How would my life have been different if I'd followed God's original plan and purpose decades earlier?*

In God's time, I mourned this lost young girl, and then rejoiced with the angels that the lost girl was found and miraculously transformed.

Other Books by Kimberly

No One Sent A Sympathy Card
The Grief that Goes Unrecognized
(A Biblical Response for Moving Beyond Life's Losses)

Turn Your Mind and Brain Back On
Unleash the Power of a Renewed Mind

Dancing In the Sonshine (Second Edition)
Restoration from the Wounds of Abuse

I'm Beautiful? Why Can't I See It? [2nd Edition]
Love Yourself and Love Your Body in 12 Weeks

Eyes Wide Open
This is a 9-weeks of *I'm Beautiful? Why Can't I See It?*

PAPA Power: *66-Days with Your Abba Father*

I'm God's Girl? Why Can't I Feel It?
Daily Biblical Encouragement to Defeat Depression & the Blues

Something Happened On My Way to Hell
Break Free from the Insatiable Pursuit of Pleasure

Breaking the Cover Girl Mask: *Toss Out Toxic Thoughts*

Deadly Love: *Confronting the Sex Trafficking of Our Children*

Foundations *(A Parent's and Youth Leader's Guide)*
Empowering Youth to Establish Healthy Sexuality & Relationships

Torn Between Two Masters
Encouraging Teens to Live Authentically in a Celebrity-Obsessed World

References

[1] Bruce D. Perry, *Born for Love* (New York: William Morrow, 2010), 129.

[2] Donna Jackson Nakazawa, *Childhood Disrupted* (NY: Atria, 2105), 15.

[3] Ibid, 24.

[4] Jesus told His disciples, *"Who has seen me has seen the Father"* *(John 14:9)*. When they looked into Jesus's face, they saw the essence of God. John's gospel states, "God is like Jesus." Sometimes the God who made the Old Testament (OT) doesn't sound like Jesus of the New Testament (NT), which can be confusing. Jesus made it clear He came to bring a new covenant; a new agreement (Luke 22:20). The God of the OT worked through the person of Jesus Christ in the NT.

[5] Stacey Colino, Health.USNews.com; August 31, 2016.

[6] James Pennebaker, University Texas, *Opening Up By Writing It Down.*

[7] Ibid, 96.

[8] Bruce D. Perry, *Born for Love* (New York: William Morrow, 2010), 162-163.

[9] Ibid, 99.

[10] Bruce D. Perry, *Born for Love* (New York: William Morrow, 2010), 38.

[11] www.westernseminary.edu/files/publications/magazine/WS_Magazine_Fall2016.pdf.

[12] Goleman, 1995; 207.

[13] Bruce D. Perry, *Born for Love* (New York: William Morrow, 2010).

[14] Donna Jackson Nakazawa, *Childhood Disrupted* (NEW YORK: Atria, 2105), 134.

[15] David Grand, *Brainspotting* (Boulder: Sounds True, 2013), 78.

[16] Francine Shapiro, *Getting Past Your Past* (New York: Rodale, 2012), 12-13.

[17] Bruce D. Perry, *Born for Love* (New York: William Morrow, 2010), 130.

[18] David Grand, *Brainspotting* (Boulder: Sounds True, 2013), 91.

[19] Ibid.

[20] Wikipedia: http://en.wikipedia.org/wiki/Mind

[21] Caroline Leaf, *Who Switched Off My Brain,* (Switch On Your Brain; 2007), 8, 113-114, 94.

[22] Levine 243

[23] Ibid, 8, 113-114, 94.

[24] Newberg and Waldman, *How God Changes Your Brain,* 39.

[25] Caroline Leaf, *Who Switched Off My Brain,* Backmatter, Switch On Your Brain Organization Pty (Ltd.), 2007

[26] Dr. Ali Binazar, *Huffington Post,* "Addiction Recovery: Why We're Addicted to Negative Behaviors," June 15, 2010.

[27] Source: Dr. Caroline Leaf; TBN, May 25, 2016

[28] Ibid.

[29] David Grand, *Brainspotting* (Boulder: Sounds True, 2013), 92.

[30] Bruce D. Perry, *Born for Love* (New York: William Morrow, 2010), 143.

[31] Louann Brizendine, *The Female Brain* (New York: Broadway Books, 2006), 128.

[32] Tim Clinton & Mark Laaser, *The Fight for Your Life,* (Destiny Image, 2015), 60.

[33] Bruce D. Perry, *Born for Love* (New York: William Morrow, 2010), 29.

[34] Rachel Goldsmith Turow, *Mindfulness Skills for Trauma and PTSD* (New York: WW Norton Company, 2017) 161.

[35] L.R. Squire and E.R. Kandel, *Memory From Mind to Molecules* (New York: Scientific American Library, 2000).

[36] Caroline Leaf, *Who Switched Off My Brain,* 113-114, Switch On Your Brain Organization Pty (Ltd.), 2007

[37] Ibid.

[38] Iyanla Vanzant, *Get Over It!* (Carlsbad: Hay House, 2018), 44.

[39] John Bargh, PhD, *Before You Know It* (NY: Touchstone, 2018), 54.

[40] Stacey Colino, Health.USNews.com; August 31, 2016.

[41] James Pennebaker, University Texas, *Opening Up By Writing It Down.*

[42] EMDR, developed by Dr. Francine Shapiro, targets unprocessed memories that contain the negative thoughts, beliefs, emotions and body sensations; Source: Francine Shapiro, *Getting Past Your Past* (New York: Rodale, 2012).

[43] David Jeremiah, *Today's Turning Point,* December 2, 2019.

[44] Norman Doidge, "On Neuroplasticity."

[45] Lisa M. Najavits, *Seeking Safety* (The Guilford Press, 2002), 289.

[46] A.W. Tozer Quotes: http://www.worldofquotes.com/author/A.w.-Tozer/1/index.html

[47] Stated in Brian F. Martin, *Invincible* (New York: Perigee, 2014), 33, 45.

[48] Caroline Leaf, "How to Protect Your Mental Health in this Current Political Climate" podcast; November 26, 2019.

[49] Mary Roach, "Can You Laugh Your Stress Away?" *Health* 10, no. 5 (September 1996), 92.

[50] Harvard Medical School Health Publishing; https://www.health.harvard.edu/staying-healthy/understanding-the-stress-response.

[51] www.ncbi.nin.nih.gove

[52] Daniel G. Amen, *Stones of Remembrance* (Carol Stream: Tyndale, 2017), 14.

[53] Ibid

[54] Michael R. Lyles, M.D., "Healthy Weight Management Strategies," *Christian Counseling Today,* 13, Vol. 16 No. 2, 2009

[55] Daniel J. DeNoon, *WebMD Health News,* "Lack of Sleep Takes Toll on Brain Power," Feb. 9, 2000

[56] Health.com, "Special Report," May 2009

[57] *Science,* October 10th issue, http://mentalhealth.about.com/b/2003/10/16/rejection-feels-like-pain-to-the-brain.htm

[58] Walt Larimore, M.D., *God's Design for the Highly Healthy Teen,* 250, Grand Rapids: Zondervan, 2005